Welcome to the World!

Carson-Dellosa's *Another Trip Around the World* gives you and your students the opportunity to explore life in Panama, Venezuela, Argentina, Antarctica, South Africa, Nigeria, Israel, Greece, Italy, France, Russia, and India. The section for each country contains basic information (area, population, flag descriptions, etc.), fascinating facts (sports, education, wildlife, etc.), language activities, recipes, classroom activities, a worksheet, flag, map, and a resource list. Below are lists of extension ideas for each type of activity provided in each country.

Basic Information

- Use Almanac information to make comparisons. For example, how many French francs will equal an American dollar?
- Discuss the different region' histories. Have the native cultures had similar experiences?
- Have the children invite their grandparents to tell stories about the history of their families' original homelands. Have them share their experiences.
- Graph the types of land formations found in each country or continent. How many have deserts, tropical zones, etc.?
- Make a list of all of the natural resources that are cultivated in each country or continent. Have your students discuss the resources in each that are imported by the United States. Can they name one from each country or continent? The students could also discuss what life would be like for our country and other countries or continents if we didn't have certain resources.
- Compare the different types of governments in each country or continent. Nations such as Russia and South Africa have undergone great political and social change. Have your students pretend they are developing a new country or continent and then choose what type of government they would like to establish in their new land.

Fascinating Facts

- Write the fascinating facts of each country or continent on 3" x 5" index cards. Laminate them. Use the cards to play a trivia game.
- Create customary art from each region described in this section. Have your students make molas, perfumed beads, coil art, dreidels, etc.
- Use the information as topics for oral or written reports. The students could even do a comparison study (sports from two countries, etc.).
- Find pictures of houses or buildings mentioned in this section or the basic information section. Assign a group of students to each country or continent. Have them build replicas with ice cream sticks, papier-mâché, grass, straw, clay, etc. Use the buildings to make a global neighborhood.

Language Activities

- Have your students create coded messages using some of each country's language. Have them pick partners and trade messages.
- Practice using the languages each day. Can the students use the words in conversation?
- Create file folder games with the different categories of words. Have the students match up all of the color words, ways to say hello, etc. (File folders can also be used to match flags, maps of countries or continents, types of money, etc.)

Recipes

- Copy the recipes in each section and send one home with each child. Have each student make the recipe with their parents and bring it to school the next day for a multicultural snack time. Host an international snack party for another class.
- Have a multicultural bake sale. Have students and their families bake their favorite international dishes. Sell the goods and donate the money raised to an international charity organization.

Classroom Activities

- Have each student make a family tree reaching as far back as possible. Post the trees around the room. Do any of the students have ancestors from any of the regions studied in this book?
- Locate schools in the regions you're studying. Contact one of the schools and see if it is willing to start a pen-pal program with your class. Contact its embassy for more information.
- Make up story starters for your class. For example, "My favorite country is ... because ...," or "I visited ..., and I saw ...."
- Host a multicultural festival with food, music, dancing, and celebrations from all of the countries or continents. Invite the whole school. Make it a yearly event.
- Research one of the regions in depth as a class. When you have gathered all the research, have your students help you put all the information into a book. Donate the book to your school library. Encourage other classrooms to do the same with other countries. Give your students assignments that will encourage them to use the books they helped make.

Worksheets

- Use the worksheets to make file folder games.
- Use the patterns to make finger puppets, necklaces, shape books, etc.

Flags

- Use the cover and flag descriptions to compare similarities in the countries' or continents' flags. How many have religious or mythical elements, how many have changed through the years, etc.?
- After studying the flag of each country, have your students pretend they are forming a new country. Have cooperative groups design samples for a flag and have them explain the reasoning behind their choice. Have the class vote on the design they want to represent their new country.
- Have a parade of nations. Have the class dress in native costumes made from fabric scraps, beads, etc. Have each child make a flag for the country or continent he is dressed to represent.
- Have each student design a flag to represent herself.
- Enlarge, reproduce, color, and mount the flags on tagboard. Post flags around the room. Borrow a copy of a national anthems record from your local library. Have the students pick a flag to salute each morning and play its anthem. You can even learn the words and sing along.
- Have a mock United Nations meeting with all of the flags and countries or continents present. Try solving global problems that are currently in the news.
- Make floor puzzles from the flags. Enlarge, color, cut out, and mount on tagboard. Cut the flag into puzzle pieces.

Maps

- Enlarge the maps to create bulletin boards or to use as pages for a shape book. On the maps, list cities, neighboring countries, natural resources, topographical regions, ethnic backgrounds, etc.
- Enlarge and trace the maps onto cardboard. Use plaster of Paris, clay, or papier-mâché to create a topographical map of the country or continent. You can add animals in appropriate places as well as natural resources and industries.

Resource List

- While studying a certain country or continent, have a student help you read one of the books each day to the class.
- Have the students pretend they are the main characters in the books. How would they react to American customs? How do they like being in the characters' shoes?
- Use the books to compare national holidays. Compare the ways other countries celebrate Easter, Christmas, Hanukkah, Diwali, etc., to how Americans celebrate similar holidays.
- Read folktales from all of the countries or continents. Discuss their similarities and differences. Have the students make up their own folktales.

First Stop...Panama

Area: 29,762 sq. miles
Capital City: Panama City
Population: 4,186,000
Main Language: Spanish
Main Religion: Roman Catholicism
Currency: Balboa
Government: Republic
Flag:

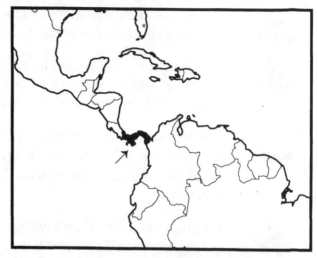

The flag of Panama was adopted in 1903. The white background stands for peace. The blue star symbolizes honesty and purity.

For Your Information

The Republic of Panama, bounded on the north by the Caribbean Sea and on the south by the Pacific Ocean, occupies the Isthmus of Panama that joins North America to South America. To the west lies Costa Rica and to the east, Colombia. Panama has a tropical climate with high humidity and heavy rainfall. The climate is also affected by altitude. Average temperatures in the lowland farming areas along the Pacific coast are around 27° C (81° F). Most of the country is covered with dense tropical forest, and animal life includes anteaters, armadillos, tapirs, small tigers, and monkeys.

The country contains a number of distinct racial and ethnic groups. Its population is classified at 70% mestizo (mixed), 14% black, 10% white, and the remaining 6% Indians and others. The most significant racial and cultural division is between the mestizo population and the blacks from Jamaica and Barbados, who were brought into the country to help construct the Panama Canal.

The Panama Canal Zone, until 1979 a United States government reservation, was a 648-square-mile area that ran through the middle of the Republic of Panama from the Atlantic to the Pacific Ocean. It extended for 5 miles on either side of the Panama Canal. Approximately 25% of the zone's territory consisted of the Gatun Lake, formed during the construction of the Panama Canal in 1912. In 1977, American President Carter and the Panamanian General Herrara negotiated two treaties calling for full Panamanian sovereignty within the zone. The zone itself was abolished in 1979.

Since the completion of the Panama Canal in 1914, Panama's economy has been greatly influenced by this world transportation artery. The canal provides revenues and jobs, and the dominant service industries function mostly near the canal. Services include an important international finance and banking sector which, along with canal tolls, has helped the Panamanian economy. The cash crops include bananas, sugar cane, and coffee. Main food crops are rice, corn, and beans.

Fascinating Facts

 Panama is like two bridges: a land link between continents (North and South America) and a sea link between oceans (the Pacific and Atlantic).

 The first European known to have visited Panama was the Spaniard Rodrigo de Bastidas in 1501. In 1502, Christopher Columbus explored the eastern Panamanian coast on his fourth trip to the New World.

 In Panama, there are three major Indian groups: the Embeni, the Guaymies, and the Kunas of the San Blas Islands off the Caribbean coast. The Kuna Indians inhabit about 50 of the 300 San Blas Islands. They farm in clearings on the mainland and harvest fish and lobster.

 Originally an Indian fishing village, Panama City is now the capital of Panama. Its name comes from the Spanish word *panama,* meaning "many fish." Panama City has become Latin America's busiest banking center. Many believe its popularity is due to the fact that the strict bank-secrecy laws lure illegal drug money. The United States forcibly removed Panamanian President Manuel Noriega in 1989 and tried him in Miami, Florida, for crimes involving drug money.

 Just east of Panama City is the city Portobelo ("beautiful port"), which was named by Christopher Columbus. It was once the greatest trade center of the New World. Now, pilgrims flock to the ruins of Portobelo for the feast of the Black Christ. The nightlong feast honors a wooden idol credited for shielding a town against cholera epidemics.

 Over the years, people from the United States called *Zonians* established communities in Panama that resemble American towns and suburbs. Two of these communities are Cristobal and Balboa.

 Construction of the Panama Canal took over ten years and cost $380,000,000. At the time of its opening, the Panama Canal was universally acknowledged as the greatest engineering feat of the modern age.

 When the canal was completed, the Canal Zone marked the historic day by placing a new motto on its official seal: "A Land Divided, The World United."

 The total length of the Panama Canal is 40 miles from shoreline to shoreline. The maximum width is about 300 feet and the maximum depth is 41 feet. Increased traffic through the Panama Canal has required the widening of the lanes. "Street lights" have been installed for night safety.

 The average toll for a ship passing through the Panama Canal is $54,000. These fees are considered well spent, for the trip through the canal saves thousands of miles and many days of travel. About 39 ships pass through the locks each day.

 Panama receives millions of dollars a month for the use of the canal. In the year 2000, Panama assumed full control over the canal. Currently, the greatest user of the Panama Canal is the United States.

Language Activities

Spanish Numbers

uno (oon-o)	one
dos (doss)	two
tres (tress)	three
cuatro (kwa-tro)	four
cinco (seen-ko)	five
seis (sseyss)	six
siete (ssyete)	seven
ocho (o-cho)	eight
nueve (nwe-be)	nine
dies (deeyes)	ten

Spanish Colors

rojo (row-ho)	red
anaranjado (a-nar-an-ha-dough)	orange
amarillo (am-a-ri-yo)	yellow
verde (vear-day)	green
azul (as-ul)	blue
rosa (row-sa)	pink
moreno (more-ai-no)	brown
negro (nay-grow)	black
blanco (bla-co)	white

Everyday Spanish Expressions

hola (OH-lah)	hello
adios (ah-DEE-ohz)	good-bye
por favor (pohr fah-VOHR)	please
gracias (GRAH-see-ahs)	thank you
Mi nombre es ... (mih NOHM-breh ehz)	My name is ...
¿Que tal? (KAY tall)	How are you?
No te preocupes. (noh teh preh-oh-KOO-pehz)	Don't worry.
Ven aquf. (vehn ah-KEE)	Come here.
¿Te puedo ayudah? (te poo-WEH-doh ah-YOO-dahr)	Can I help?

Panamanian Poem

Los pollitos dicen,	The little chicks say,
"Pio, pio, pio,"	"Cheep, cheep, cheep,"
Cuando tienen hambre	When they're hungry and
Cuando tienen frio.	When they're cold.

Panamanian Recipes

Empanadas (Meat-Filled Turnovers)

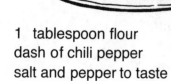

Ingredients:

¼ pound ground beef
1 medium onion diced
1 green pepper diced
1 clove garlic diced
1 teaspoon sugar

1 tablespoon flour
dash of chili pepper
salt and pepper to taste
8 frozen ready-made pie crusts, thawed

Directions:
Heat oven to 400°. In a large skillet, cook ground beef thoroughly and drain. Gradually add the next 8 ingredients. Cover and simmer for 15 minutes. While beef mixture is cooling, use a glass to cut a pie crust circle for each student. Place the small circles of pie crust on large ungreased cookie sheets. Spoon approximately 1 teaspoon of ground beef mixture into the center of each pie crust circle. Fold the pie crust, forming a half-circle, and press edges down with a fork to seal the crust together. Bake for 10-15 minutes or until golden brown.

Sopa de Gloria

Ingredients:

1 quart + 2 tablespoons water
1 large can sweetened condensed milk
1 large can evaporated milk
2 tablespoons cornstarch
pinch of salt
3 or 4 cinnamon sticks

3 eggs
1 tablespoon vanilla
2 eight-inch sponge cakes
½ pound sugar
½ teaspoon almond extract

Directions:
Put the water, condensed milk, evaporated milk, cornstarch, salt, and cinnamon sticks together in a heavy saucepan. Bring to a boil, stirring constantly, then simmer on low heat for 10 minutes. Separate the egg whites from the yolks. Stir the yolks in a cup and add 2 tablespoons of water. Remove the milk mixture from the heat and add the egg yolks, stirring well. Add vanilla and let cool. While the milk mixture is cooling, cut the sponge cakes in small pieces, 2" long and 1" wide, and place in a glass baking dish. Cover the sponge cake pieces thoroughly with the cooled milk mixture. Beat egg whites, gradually adding sugar until thick, then beat in the almond extract. Cover the sponge cake pieces and milk mixture with the egg whites and place in an oven for 2 to 3 minutes to brown slightly. Remove from oven and let cool. Chill cakes in the refrigerator before serving.

Classroom Activities

The land of Panama is called an *isthmus* (a narrow strip of land, bordered on both sides by water, connecting two larger bodies of land). The Panama Canal cuts through Panama and is important economically to the country. Using several maps and globes, have your children look for other isthmuses in the world. Is there another place on the globe where a strategic canal has been or could be placed?

Tropical fruits, such as papayas, mangos, coconuts and bananas, are common foods of Panama. Have a fruit-tasting party with your students. Let your students compare and contrast common American fruits to those from Panama.

Quince Años, the fifteenth birthday or "coming of age," is extravagantly celebrated in Panama. Families will often rent ballrooms and have elaborate decorations and gifts for the birthday child. Have your students decide what special birthday age they would like to celebrate in the United States and then describe how they would make it special.

The province of Darien in eastern Panama borders Colombia. Darien is the largest and least developed area of Panama. Jungles are abundant with a large variety of plants and animals. Some of the large animals include the red deer, tapir, alligator, puma, agouti, ocelot, margay, and wild boar. Have your students select an animal indigenous to Darien and research the animal in your school's library. Students can write several facts and draw a simple sketch of the animal.

The Kuna Indians of the San Blas Islands create brightly-colored, appliqued fabric panels called *molas.* Molas are an important part of the everyday costume of the Kuna women, and they are often used as wall hangings, jewelry, coasters, and holiday ornaments. Create greeting cards or a colorful bulletin board by making molas. After students make their own molas following the directions below, give them copies of the activity on page 8 to color.

Draw and cut a simple shape (plant, animal, person, or abstract design) from brightly colored construction paper or fabric. Glue the design to another piece of construction paper or fabric. Cut around the edge of the shape about ¼" away from the original line. Glue the design onto yet another piece of paper or fabric. Repeat several times until you have three to five layers. Finally, glue the mola to a contrasting piece of construction paper.

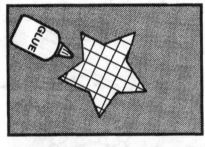
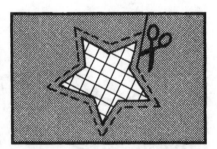

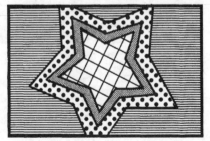

Name _____

San Blas Children of Panama

Directions: Color the San Blas Island natives below. Their traditional dress should be brightly colored.

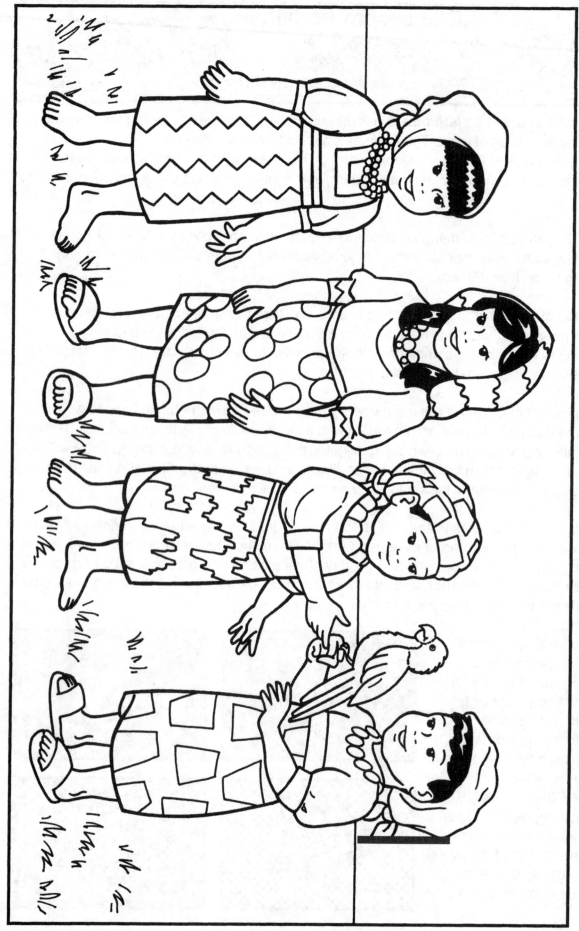

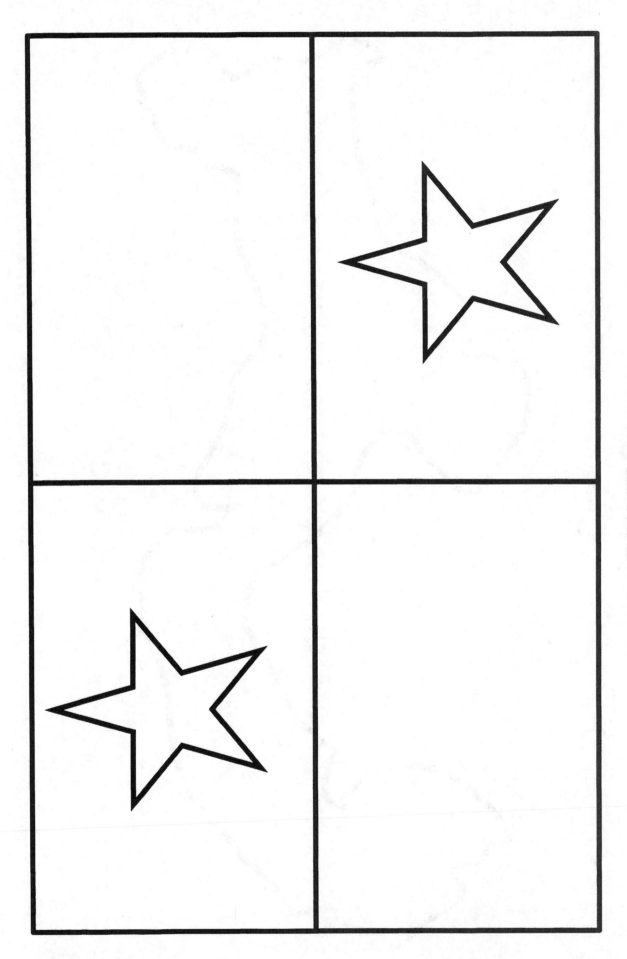

The Flag of Panama

Panama

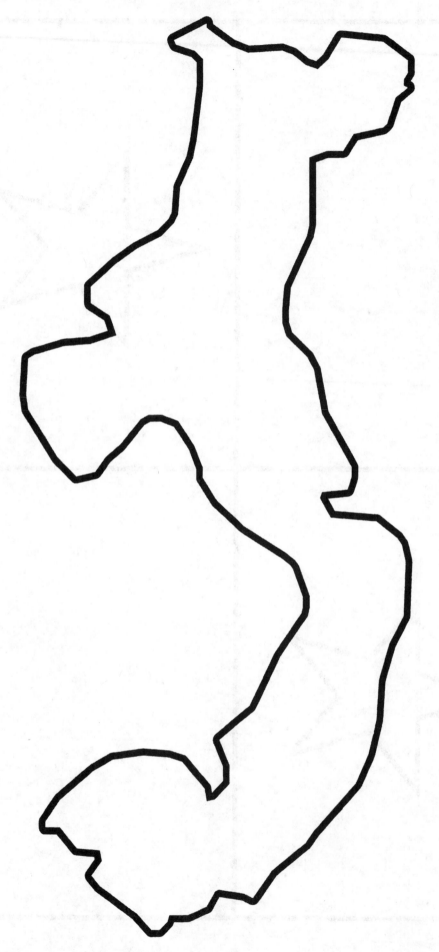

Teacher Resources

Augustin, Byron. *Panama.* Children's Press, 2005.

Dolan, Edward F. *Panama and the United States: Their Canal, Their Stormy Years.* Franklin Watts, 1990.

DuTemple, Lesley. *The Panama Canal.* Lerner Publishing Group, 2002.

Griffiths, John. *Take a Trip to Panama.* Franklin Watts, 1989.

Mann, Elizabeth. *The Panama Canal (Wonders of the World* Series). Mikaya Press, 1998.

Markun, Patricia Maloney. *The Little Painter of Sabana Grande.* Bradbury Press, 1993.

Markun, Patricia Maloney. *It's Panama's Canal!* Linnet Books, 1999.

Nobleman, Marc Tyler. *Panama (Countries of the World* Series). Bridgestone Books, 2002.

Rau, Dana Meachen. *Panama.* Children's Press, 1999.

Stein, R. Conrad. *The Story of the Panama Canal.* Children's Press, 1982.

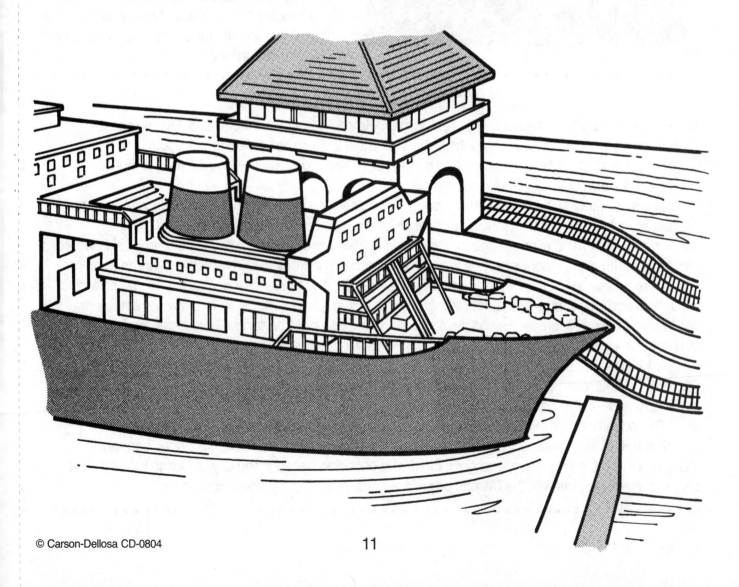

Next Stop...Venezuela

Area: 352,144 sq. miles
Capital City: Caracas
Population: 31,568,179
Main Language: Spanish
Main Religion: Roman Catholicism
Currency: Bolivar
Government: Federal Republic
Flag:

The flag of Venezuela was adopted in 1954. The tricolor flag is yellow, blue, and red. The blue stripe in the middle has seven pointed white stars forming an arch.

For Your Information

The most northerly South American nation, Venezuela has a long Caribbean and Atlantic coast on the north and east. Bordering republics are Colombia to the west, Brazil to the south, and Guyana to the east. Lightly populated and mineral rich, Venezuela has enjoyed a free, populist democracy since 1958.

Approximately 10% of Venezuela's people are classified as black and 2% as Native American; the rest are white or mestizo. Heavy immigration and a high birthrate have contributed to rapid population growth. The average age in Venezuela is 25.6. Venezuela's varied topography and climate provide a number of ecological zones for flora and fauna. The tropical rain forests are home to animals such as monkeys, boa constrictors, anacondas, alligators, and freshwater dolphins and plants such as orchids and mahogany and rubber trees. The savannas have armadillos, capybaras, anteaters, and sloths. The more temperate coastal range and valleys have foxes, rabbits, pumas, and the deadly bushmaster snake as well as acacia, palm, poinsettias, and other flowering shrubs.

A 1980 law extended the number of years of compulsory primary schooling from six to nine. Still, only an estimated one out of every three students completes primary school, and only about 9% of the appropriate age group attends a university.

The country is rich in mineral resources, especially petroleum reserves, including the heavy oil belt of the Orinoco Basin. There are significant deposits of iron, bauxite, coal, copper, diamonds, nickel, manganese, and gold. Gold was only discovered in the city of Callao in 1940. The southern river systems, like the Caroni, provide a major source of hydroelectric power.

Fascinating Facts

 Spanish explorers came to northern Venezuela in the fifteenth century. There, they found Indians living in homes built on wooden stilts over a huge yet shallow lake called Lake Maracaibo. Reminded of the homes built along the canals of Venice, Italy, explorers named the region **Venezuela**, Spanish for "Little Venice."

 The world's largest oil fill is in Lake Maracaibo, Venezuela. Oil has changed Venezuela from a poor farming nation into a prosperous spendthrift nation almost overnight. However, a large debt and lower oil prices are forcing Venezuela to reduce its dependence on oil.

 Although Venezuela is one of the wealthiest countries in South America (mainly due to its large deposits of oil), only 5% of its population controls 90% of its land and resources.

 Venezuela is located entirely within the tropics; however, due to its high altitude, some mountain peaks remain permanently snow-capped.

 Caracas, the capital and most important city in Venezuela, is busy, bustling, and populous. Traffic jams have become so severe in Caracas that drivers must leave their cars at home one day a week.

 Over 900 species of orchids grow in Venezuela. Some orchids in the country are so small (the size of pinheads), they can only be fertilized by one species of insect.

 Llaneros are Venezuelan cowboys. They invented a sport called bull-tossing. A llanero catches a fast-running bull and twists its tail to make the animal fall to the ground. Baseball and soccer are also popular sports.

 Capybara, the world's largest rodents (4 feet long, 110 pounds), live in the rivers and swamps of Venezuela's rain forest.

 The highest waterfall in the world, Angel Falls, is in Venezuela. It was discovered by an American pilot, Jimmy Angel, in 1935. Angel Falls, at 3,212 feet, is fifteen times higher than Niagara Falls.

 Many Venezuelan children have hot chocolate for breakfast. The hot chocolate is very thick, like a soupy pudding. Often the children will dip bread in their drink.

Christmas is gaily celebrated in Venezuela. Children wait for *Niño Jesus* ("Baby Jesus") to bring them gifts. In some towns, children tie strings to their big toes at bedtime and the ends hang out the windows. The next morning, friends pull the strings to wake up the children.

It is bad manners for adults to eat on the street. Also, pointing with the index finger can be considered rude. Motioning with the entire hand is more polite.

Language Activities

Venezuelan Poems

Aaroz con leche

Aaroz con leche
Me quiero casar
Con una ninita de la capital.
Que sepa caser.
Que sepa bordar.
Que sepa abrir la puerta
Para ira jugar.

Rice with Milk

Rice with milk
I want to get married
With a girl from the capital city.
She knows how to sew.
She knows how to embroider.
She knows how to open the door
To go out to play.

Qué llueva

(Sung to the tune of
"It's Raining, It's Pouring")
Qué llueva
Qué llueva
La bruja está en la cueva
Los pajaritos cantan
Los niños se levantan.

It's Raining

It's raining
It's raining
The witch is in the cave
The little birds are singing
The children all stand up.

Un elefante se balanceaba (from
a traditional counting rhyme in
Spanish)

Un elefante
se balanceaba
sabre la tela
de una arana,
como vefa
que resistra
fue a llamar
a otro elefante.

Dos elefantes
se balanceaban ...

Tres elefantes ...

One Little Elephant
(from a traditional counting rhyme
in English)

One little elephant,
Out for a run,
Climbed up a spider's web
Just for fun.
He tiptoed across,
He did a little dance,
And then he called down
For some *more* ele-phants.

Two little elephants,
Out for a run ...

Three little elephants ...

Pan de Jamón (Ham Bread)

Ingredients:
canned pizza crust
butter or margarine
1   package of ham slices
½ cup chopped green olives
½   cup raisins
egg white

Directions:
Unroll the pizza crust on a clean, flat surface.
Spread the crust evenly with butter or margarine.
Place ham slices over the butter or margarine.
Sprinkle with olives and raisins. Roll up the crust
and flatten the ends. Brush rolled crust with the
egg white. Place in a bread pan, seam side down.
Bake for 30 minutes at 350°.

Quesillo (Little Cheesecake)

Ingredients:
½ cup sugar
⅛ cup water
4   eggs
1   can evaporated milk
1   can sweetened, condensed milk
1 teaspoon vanilla

Directions:
In an ovenproof pan, boil the sugar and water,
tilting the pan to coat. Do not brown. Mix the
remaining ingredients in a blender. Pour the
mixture into the caramelled pan. Refrigerate, then
bake for 1 hour at 350° or until a knife inserted into
the quesillo comes out clean.

Classroom Activities

Using a large piece of tagboard, have your students work in cooperative groups to create a travel poster or postcard to lure tourists to Venezuela. On the back of the tagboard, students can write several facts about the country.

Venezuelans are very patriotic and extremely proud of the Venezuelan hero, Simon Bolivar, known as ''The Liberator'' of South America. Have your students discuss and write about an American hero and tell why the person is important to them.

The coastline of Venezuela extends for 1,750 miles along the Caribbean Sea on the north and the Atlantic Ocean on the east. Tropical fish are plentiful in the Caribbean waters. Have your students complete the activity on page 17 and display the colorful tropical fish of Venezuela in your classroom for a bright bulletin board.

Using shoe boxes, let your students make dioramas of the typical dwellings in the large cities or the countryside of Venezuela. Your students may want to show the contrast of houses of the very rich and the very poor.

Create a floor map of Venezuela with a white shower curtain liner. Outline the country using an opaque or overhead projector. Physical features such as mountains, plains, and lakes as well as cities and other points of interest can be constructed from colored paper. Attach the features with self-stick hook and fastener tape (such as Velcro brand). Students can use a map of Venezuela to replace the pieces in a learning center.

Ceramics are a common folk craft in Venezuela and are made by both artists and school children. Have your students use red clay that can be fired in a kiln to create their own ceramics, such as jars, bowls, or small wall-hangings in the shapes of suns or fish. As an alternative, follow the ceramic dough recipe below and let the finished products thoroughly dry in the sun. When dry, students can paint their creations.

Ceramic Dough
Ingredients:
4 cups salt
$1\frac{1}{3}$ cups + 1 cup water
2 cups cornstarch

Directions:
Mix the salt and $1\frac{1}{3}$ cups of water in a pan. Thoroughly heat the mixture on a stove, stirring constantly (3 to 4 minutes). Remove from heat. Mix together the corn starch and remaining cup of water. Quickly add to the first mixture and stir well. The mixture should be a stiff dough. (If it does not thicken, reheat and stir for one more minute.)

Name _____

Tropical Fish of Venezuela

Use the color code to color the parts of the tropical fish.

purple -- cities in Venezuela	blue -- plants	yellow -- animals	green -- bordering countries

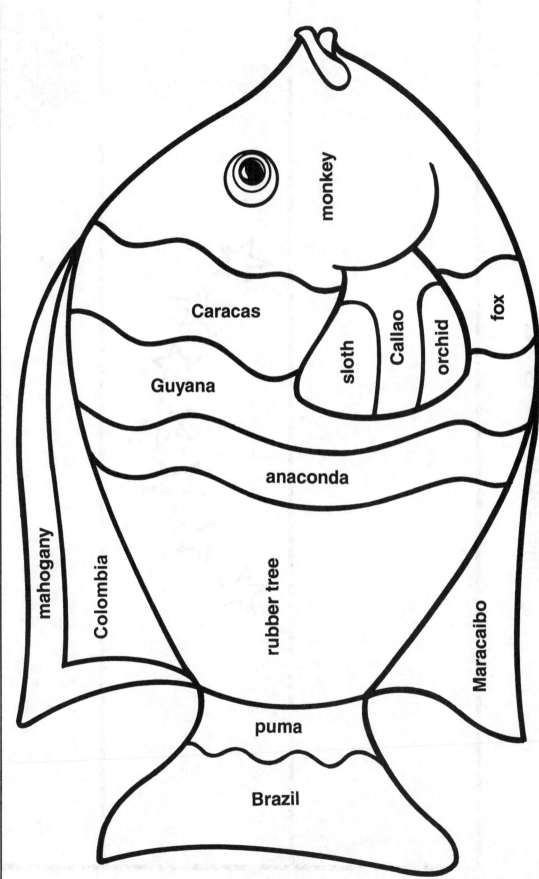

monkey

Caracas

sloth

Callao

orchid

fox

Guyana

anaconda

mahogany

Colombia

rubber tree

Maracaibo

puma

Brazil

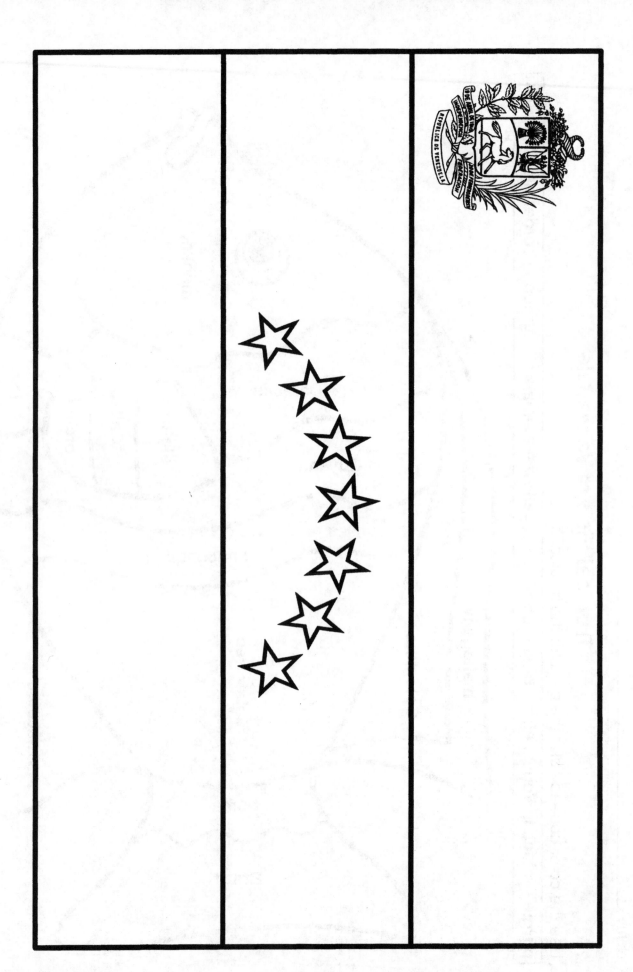

The Flag of Venezuela

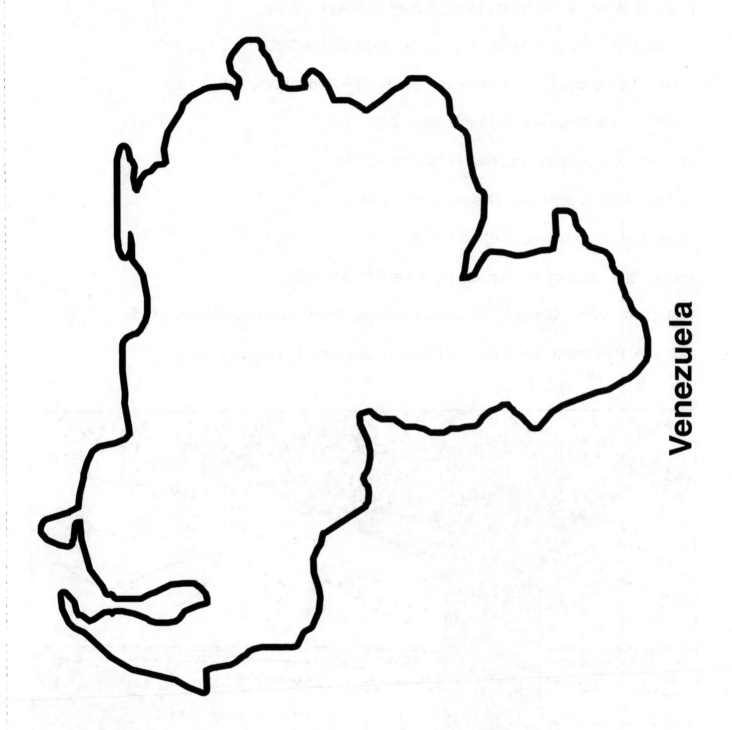

Venezuela

Teacher Resources

Aalgaard, Wendy. *Venezuela in Pictures.* Lerner Publications, 2004.

Fox, Geoffrey. *Land and People of Venezuela.* HarperCollins Children's Books, 1991.

George, Jean Craighead. *One Day in the Tropical Rain Forest.* HarperTrophy, 1995.

Heinrichs, Ann. *Venezuela.* Children's Press, 1997.

Lye, Keith. *Take a Trip to Venezuela.* Franklin Watts, 1988.

Morrison, Marion. *Venezuela.* Chelsea House, 1998.

Weeks, Morris. *Hello Venezuela.* Norton, 1968.

Wilcox, John. *Traveling in Venezuela.* Hippocrene Books, 1980.

Winter, Jane Kohen. *Venezuela (Cultures of the World Series).* Benchmark Books, 2002.

Wohlrabe, Raymond A. *The Land and People of Venezuela.* Lippincott, 1963.

Arriving in Argentina

Area: 1,068,302 sq. miles
Capital City: Buenos Aires
Population: 44,293,293
Main Language: Spanish
Main Religion: Roman Catholicism
Currency: Peso
Government: Republic
Flag:

Adopted in 1818, the flag's coat of arms bears a sun, which represents Argentina's freedom from Spain. The colors blue and white are worn by patriots who fought off the British invaders in 1806-1807.

For Your Information

Argentina, the second largest country in Latin America, occupies most of the southern portion of the South American continent. Argentina is bordered by five countries: Chile to the west, Bolivia and Paraguay to the north, and Brazil and Uruguay to the northeast. Argentina is the third most populous country in Latin America (after Brazil and Mexico), having about 7% of the region's total population. Argentina is one of the more highly developed countries in the Western Hemisphere.

The country's economy has gradually shifted from an exclusive dependence on the large-scale production of livestock and agricultural goods to one in which the industrial and service sectors are now dominant. Since the 1950s, it has been one of the world's principal trading nations. Argentina has a varied base of mineral deposits, but most are small and are in remote regions of the Andes or Patagonia. Petroleum is the only mineral produced in a substantial quantity, and about 21 million metric tons (over 23 million U.S. tons) are extracted each year, making Argentina nearly self-sufficient in liquid fuels.

Most Argentinians are descendants of either the Spaniards who settled in the 16th century or the millions of European immigrants who arrived in the late 19th and 20th centuries. The mestizo (mixed Indian and European) and Indian populations, once a majority, have been absorbed into the general population, and as a distinct ethnic group now number only about 30,000.

Animal life in Argentina is especially rich and varied. Llama and vicuna inhabit the Andean tracts, while jaguars, pumas, monkeys, deer, foxes, and wild boars are found at lower elevations. Birds, including the condor, and fish are particularly numerous, and the country is one of the richest in dinosaur fossils.

Fascinating Facts

 Argentina gets its name from the Latin word **argentum,** meaning "silver." Early Spanish explorers hoped to find silver as they explored the new land. Unfortunately for them, they were disappointed.

 Early Indians from the Patagonia region of Argentina were almost six feet tall and looked even larger because they wore thick furs to keep warm. European explorers in the 1500s named the land Patagonia or "land of the big feet" because the Indians' feet looked huge. The Indians actually stuffed grass in their boots to keep warm.

 Argentine beef is world famous, and cattle ranching is one of the biggest industries in Argentina. In the cities, restaurants have special grills called **parrillas,** where thick, juicy steaks are cooked to order at very reasonable prices.

 Unlike many other South American countries, there are not immense differences between the very rich and the very poor. Most Argentines refer to themselves as middle class. However, there are some unfriendly differences between the city dwellers of Buenos Aires who call themselves **porteños** (people of the port) and the **caudillos** (people of the countryside).

 The tango dance of Argentina is one of the best known Latin American popular dances. The word **tango** comes from the name of a drum used by black slaves. Next to the tango, opera is the most popular music in Argentina. Teatro Colon in Buenos Aires is one of the world's greatest opera houses. The main stage of the Colon is over one block long!

 Argentina is home to the world's widest waterfall, **Iguazu Falls.** Acquiring its name from the Indian words for "great waters," Iguazu Falls is over two miles wide and is a spectacular tourist attraction.

 Argentines love to read; the literacy rate is over 97%. The constitution of Argentina protects freedom of the press, but only in the provinces. Although there are over 10 daily newspapers in Buenos Aires, the press must constantly be careful not to offend the authorities. Under President Juan Peron (from 1946-55 and 1973-74) and other presidents, newspapers could be shut down quickly if they offended the leaders of the country.

 Almost all children can read or write even in the remote regions of the country. President Domingo Sarmiento, who ruled Argentina from 1868 to 1874, was a leader in promoting high standards of education. There are not enough state primary and secondary schools to teach all of the children at the same time. Students go to school either in the morning or in the afternoon.

 The rough-and-tumble game of **pato** originated with the gaucho cowboys of Argentina. In the old days, a live duck (**pato** in Spanish) was stuffed into a sack with only its head sticking out. Two teams of horsemen would fight over the sack, tossing it back and forth over a three-mile-long field. Today, however, the game is played with a large ball with six handles. Players try to stuff the ball into a large net in order to score points.

Argentine Poem

El Reino del Reves by
María Elena Walsh

Me dijeron que en el Reino del Reves
Nada el pajaro y vuela el pez,
Que los gatos no hacen miau
y dicen "yes" porque ostudian mucho ingles.
Vamos a ver como es el Rei no del Reves.

Me dijeron que en el Reino del Reves
nadie baila con los pies
que un raton es vigilante,
y otro es juez;
y que dos y dos son tres.
Vamos a ver como es el Reino del Reves.

Me dijeron que en el Reino del Reves
cabe un oso en una nuez,
que usau tacos y bigotes los bebes
y que un ano dura un mes.
Vamos a ver como es el Rei no del Reves.

Me dijeron que en el Reino del Reves
hay un perro pekines
quese cae para arriba y que una vez
no pudo bajar despues.
Vamos a ver como es el Rei no del Reves.

Me dijeron que en el Reino del Reves
un senora llamado Andres,
tiene 1500 chimpances que si miras
no los ves.
Vamos a ver como es el Reino del Reves.

Me dijeron que en el Reino del Reves
una arana y un cienpies
van anudados al palacio del marques
en caballeos de ajedrez.
Vamos a ver como es el Reino del Reves.

Kingdom of Reverse (Backwards)
(Translation by Jim Volkema)

I was told that in the Kingdom of Reverse
There are swimming cats and flying fish,
The cats don't cry out loud
And call out "yes" learning English in their test.
Let's see what goes on in the Kingdom of Reverse.

I was told that in the Kingdom of Reverse
No one dances on their feet.
One rat is the night watchman,
The other a judge;
And that two plus two is three.
Let's see what goes on in the Kingdom of Reverse.

I was told that in the Kingdom of Reverse
A bear fits in a nut,
The kids are grown-ups, and little girls wear makeup
And a week feels like a year.
Let's see what goes on in the Kingdom of Reverse.

I was told that in the Kingdom of Reverse
There is a cute Pekinese
That falls up
And gets lost flying down.
Let's see what goes on in the Kingdom of Reverse.

I was told that in the Kingdom of Reverse
That a lady was named Andrew,
That she has 1500 chimpanzees
And if you look, there is not a chimp to be seen.
Let's see what goes on in the Kingdom of Reverse.

I was told in the Kingdom of Reverse
That a spider and a centipede
Talk of love and play the fiddle
Riding the chess board.
Let's see what goes on in the Kingdom of Reverse.

Argentine Recipes

Argentine Butter Cookies

Ingredients:
2 cups sugar
1½ cup butter, softened
2 eggs
4 egg yolks
4 teaspoons grated lemon rind

2 tablespoons vanilla extract
3 cups flour
1 cup cornstarch
2 teaspoons baking powder

Directions:
Combine the sugar and butter in a large bowl. Stir until completely mixed. Add the eggs and egg yolks, stirring until light and fluffy. Add the lemon rind and vanilla. Stir in the flour, cornstarch, and baking powder. Mix thoroughly. Roll the dough onto a floured board and cut out cookies with a small glass. Bake on a greased cookie sheet at 325° for 8-10 minutes or until golden brown. Make a cookie sandwich with *dulce de leche* (see below).

Dulce de Leche (Sweet Milk Dessert)

Ingredients:
2 cans of sweetened, condensed milk
ice cream or butter cookies

Directions:
Shake the cans of condensed milk. Place the unopened cans in a saucepan and cover completely with water. Boil the cans for 1½ hours, making sure that the cans are always covered with water. Open the cans when completely cool and pour the butterscotch-type sauce over ice cream or spread between two butter cookies.

Argentine Steak Marinade

Argentina is famous for its wonderful beef. Make this marinade at school, then divide it among your students to take home for a delicious steak dinner. The recipe can be doubled if desired.

Ingredients:
4 cloves garlic finely chopped
1 cup vegetable oil
½ cup white wine vinegar
½ cup lemon juice
¼ cup parsley
1 teaspoon crushed red pepper

Directions:
Mix all of the ingredients together and pour over the meat.
Cover and refrigerate for 4 hours, turning meat occasionally.

Classroom Activities

Argentina's flag is fun to paint! Put the following in a classroom center: 12" x 18" white construction paper and yellow and light blue tempera paint. Let the students copy the flag from a book or from the outline on page 27 and then paint it. When dry, students can write facts about Argentina on the backs of their flags.

The tango dance originated in Argentina. Invite a local dance group or dance teacher to introduce your students to the popular Latin American dance. Students can also create their own movements to the distinctive music.

For hundred of years, the Falkland Islands (also known as **Islas Malvinas** in Argentina) have been the center of territorial debates. The islands have been a British colony since the beginning of the 19th century. Argentina's military rulers, however, decided that British occupation was an insult to their national dignity. In 1982, Argentina invaded the islands but after several months of land and sea battles, the British pushed the Argentines off the islands. Have students divide into two groups and debate which country, Britain or Argentina, should have control over the Falkland Islands.

Have your students work in cooperative groups to compare their state, region or country to Argentina. Students can look up the average weather conditions, city sizes, populations, area, geography, popular sports, etc. They can use chart paper to present the information to the class as if they were travel agents preparing a trip to Argentina.

Eat Argentina! Using a large sugar cookie cut in the shape of Argentina and a variety of edible goodies, let your students work in groups to create a fun and delicious topographical map. For example, use white frosting for adhesive and top with cone-shaped corn snacks for mountains, green gumdrops for hills, brown sugar for deserts, sugar-colored blue for rivers, etc.

Play Spanish Bingo. Duplicate the BINGO card on page 26 for each student. Write the Spanish words from the list below in the squares of each BINGO card. Give each student a copy of the translation list below. A caller calls out the words in English. Players cover the squares with the Spanish equivalents with playing chips until one person covers a straight line of squares (horizontally, vertically, or diagonally) and calls out "BINGO!"

hola-hello
si-yes
no-no
amigo-friend
muy bien-good
por favor-please
gracias-thank you
mí-me
tu-you
aquí-here

mamá-mother
papá-father
buenas dias-good day
lunes-Monday
martes-Tuesday
miércoles-Wednesday
jeuves-Thursday
viernes-Friday
sábado-Saturday
domingo-Sunday

uno-one
dos-two
tres-three
cuatro-four
cinco-five
seis-six
siete-seven
ocho-eight
nueve-nine
dies-ten

Name_____

B I N G O

		GRATIS		

The Flag of Argentina

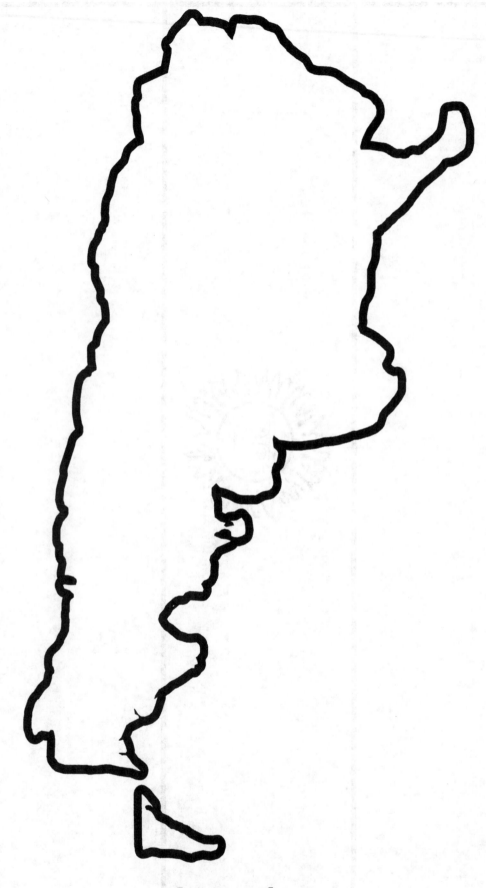

Argentina

Teacher Resources

Brusca, Maria Cristina. *On the Pampas.* Henry Holt, 1993.

Brusca, Maria Cristina. *My Mama's Little Ranch on the Pampas.* Henry Holt, 1994.

Burgan, Michael. *Argentina.* Children's Press, 1999.

Englar, Mary. *Argentina: A Question and Answer Book.* Capstone Press, 2005.

Gofen, Ethel. *Argentina (Cultures of the World Series).* Benchmark Books, 2002.

Hall, Elvajean. *The Land and People of Argentina.* HarperCollins Children's Books, 1972.

Hintz, Martin. *Argentina (Enchantment of the World Series).* Children's Press, 1998.

Huber, Alex. *We Live in Argentina.* Hodder Wayland, 1984.

Jacobsen, Karen. *Argentina (A New True Book).* Children's Press, 1990.

Liebowitz, Sol. *Argentina (Places and Peoples of the World Series).* Chelsea House, 1997.

Lye, Keith. *Take a Trip to Argentina.* Franklin Watts, 1986.

Peterson, Marge and Peter. *Argentina: A Wild West Heritage.* Dillon Press, 1990.

On to Antarctica

Area: 5,500,000 sq. miles
Capital City: None
Population: Varies
Main Language: None
Main Religion: None
Currency: None
Government: None
Flag:

Antarctica does not have an official flag. Use the flag outline on page 36 to let students design their own Antarctic flags.

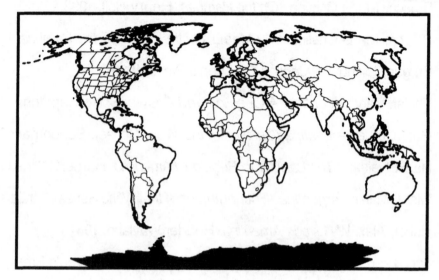

For Your Information

Antarctica, which is twice the size of the United States, is the fifth largest and southernmost continent. Its position at the South Pole, together with its elevation and ice-and-snow cover, makes Antarctica the coldest place on Earth. Its gigantic ice sheet covers all but 2 to 3 percent of Antarctica and extends over the encircling ocean. In striking contrast to the ice cover are the "dry valley" areas of the continent, especially in Victoria Land, which receives little snowfall.

The summer population is several thousand, but only a few hundred scientists stay during the winter. They live in semipermanent bases, the largest of which is the United States' base at McMurdo, Ross Island.

Most of the life on and around the Antarctic continent is supported by the sea because the continent itself is barren. Life on land consists primarily of a few species of lichens and mosses; some small floating plants called phytoplankton, which occur in certain freshwater lakes in ice-free desert areas; and a few arthropods, the most numerous of which are several groups of mites. The sea, on the other hand, is extremely rich in life because in many areas water movement is vertical, bringing nutrients from the bottom to the surface. Several species of zooplankton are important to the Antarctic marine ecosystem; however, krill is usually recognized as the most important. These small, shrimp-like organisms feed directly on various small plants and are in turn the primary food source for penguins, seals, whales and fish in the Antarctic area. Krill are the ocean's largest single source of protein.

Due to the exploitation of certain Antarctic species, several agreements to conserve Antarctica's living resources have been signed. The Antarctic Treaty states specifically that Antarctica shall be used for peaceful purposes only and supports the freedom of scientific investigation and teamwork.

Fascinating Facts

Antarctica is the coldest, highest, and windiest place on earth. The coldest temperature ever recorded in the world was here, 127° below zero! In the winter (March to September), the extreme cold causes Antarctica to double in size due to sea ice.

Antarctica receives so little precipitation it is considered the world's largest desert! It receives only about five inches of snow per year. It is so cold, the snow never melts.

More than two-thirds of the world's fresh water is frozen in Antarctic ice. In some places the ice is over 10,000 feet thick. If the ice melted, the oceans throughout the world would rise and flood all the coastal areas.

Although there is not a tree, bush, or blade of grass on the entire frozen continent of Antarctica, it does have an active volcano named Mount Erebus.

In the Antarctic summer (December to February), the sun shines 24 hours a day, but the temperature seldom reaches freezing. Goggles or protective glasses are worn during the daylight hours in Antarctica. Snow blindness may result for 2-5 days when eye protection is not used.

Millions of years ago, Antarctica was a warm, ice free land covered with trees and other plants. Fossils of plants and animals verify this fact.

No one owns Antarctica. In 1959, 12 nations signed a treaty agreeing that Antarctica should be used for peaceful purposes and scientific research. Many people believe Antarctica should be further protected as a world park.

Antarctica could be named the "Penguin Capital of the World" because millions of penguins live there. Only two species, the Adélie and the Emperor penguins, live on Antarctica year-round.

Penguins are social animals living and playing together in colonies called *rookeries.* Some of the rookeries have over one million penguins. The sound made by so many penguins chattering and fighting can be deafening.

All penguins are flightless, using their wings to swim rather than fly. Their wings, called "flippers," are more like paddles that swing back and forth to propel the penguins through water. Most penguins can swim at a speed of about 15 miles per hour!

Penguins are very good parents. When a female penguin lays an egg, the father penguin balances the egg on his feet under a thick flap of skin to keep the egg warm. He does this for six weeks while the mother travels to the sea to feed. The mother returns as the egg is ready to hatch, and the egg is carefully passed to the mother as the father goes to feed. By this time, he has lost nearly half his body weight. After the egg hatches, the adult penguins partially digest their food (krill) so that they can bring it up again to feed the baby penguin.

Way Down South

Way down south in a cold and windy land,
There are no trees, no bushes, no sand.
It's a continent of ice with penguins and seals
That swim in the ocean feeding on krill.
Antarctica's the place where scientists go
To explore the frozen desert and teach us
What they know.

Five Little Penguins

Five little penguins floating on the ice.
The first dove in. "My, the water's nice!"
The second one said, "Let's go for a swim."
The third one said, "I'll be right in."
The fourth one said, "It looks like so much fun."
The last one said, "No way! I'll stay in the sun."

I'm a Little Penguin

I'm a little penguin
Just a few days old,
Trying to keep warm
In the Antarctic cold.
Mom and Dad care for me
By giving me heat.
Watch me as I sit upon
Their nice warm feet.

Elegant Penguins

We penguins are so elegant
With built-in shirt and built-in pants.
We stand so tall and confident.
We penguins are so elegant.

We penguins are so elegant
With built-in shirt and built-in pants.
We look splendid and flamboyant.
We penguins are so elegant.

We penguins are so elegant
With built-in shirt and built-in pants.
We simply look magnificent.
We penguins are so elegant.

No country owns Antarctica; therefore, Antarctica does not have an official flag. Have your students use copies of page 36 to create their own flags for the continent. Students can take turns explaining why they used specific pictures, colors, and symbols.

Imagine with your students that you are going to take a three-day field trip to Antarctica. In cooperative groups, have the children decide the route they will travel and what clothes and supplies they will need to bring along. Remember: it is extremely cold and windy in Antarctica and there are no stores or gas stations for food and fuel.

Throughout the waters surrounding Antarctica, there are icebergs. Some are as tall as mountains! However, most of an iceberg (90%) is under water. This makes it very dangerous for ships traveling through an area where icebergs are found. Try this "Tip of the Iceberg" experiment with your class. Fill a glass container almost full of water. Drop in a large ice cube. Have your students observe the little "iceberg" and draw what they see.

For a fun snack, make "Penguin Food" with your class. Mix together two packages of fish-shaped pretzels, three cups of raisins, three cups of puffed cereal, and two cups of colorful candy-covered chocolates. Divide the snack among your students and serve it with an ice-cold drink.

Although few animals live in the Antarctic, those that do are very interesting. Have your students write simple Antarctic animal reports using a six-page flip book (see the directions below). Some animals that children may want to research include: krill, penguins (Emperor, Adélie), seals (leopard, Weddell, elephant, crabeater), the tern, and the skua. Let your students share their information with the class, and you can encourage the use of a visual aid such as a poster or diorama.

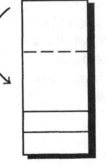

Directions:
1. Stagger three pages of paper.

2. Fold one end over to create six flaps. Staple at the top.

3. Put the title on the first flap and fill out the remaining five flaps with questions.

4. Students will lift each flap to complete the information.

Adélie Penguins

What do they look like?

Where do they live?

What do they eat?

They are interesting because...

If I had one for a pet, I would...

33

Penguin Art Projects

Be An Elegant Penguin

Your students can dress like penguins with this simple costume.

Materials:

large paper grocery bag	scissors
black tempera paint	glue
construction paper (white, black, orange)	yarn
	paintbrush

Directions:

Have students paint the bag entirely black. Cut out a belly from white paper and glue the belly to the bag. Cut a hole in the bag's bottom large enough to accommodate a child's head. To create armholes and flippers, cut rounded flaps from the side panels. Make a penguin mask from black paper and cut out two holes for the eyes. Cut a beak from orange paper and glue it to the mask. Tie the mask on using yarn. It is fun to wear the penguin costumes as students recite the poem "Elegant Penguins" from page 32.

A Perky Penguin

Materials:
empty 2-liter plastic
  soda bottle
medium plastic foam
  egg
black spray paint
glue
white paper (belly)
black paper (wings)
yellow paper (feet)
orange paper (beak)
large wiggly eyes
scissors

Directions:

Spray paint the bottle and the plastic foam egg black. Glue or press on the egg for the head. Cut an oval penguin's belly from white paper and glue to the front of the bottle. Cut out wings from black paper and feet from yellow paper. Form a cone-shaped beak from orange paper. Attach the wings, feet, and beak with glue. Last, add the eyes to have your own "Perky Penguin!"

A "Rookery of Penguins" Bulletin Board

Materials:
black marker or crayon
paper plate
cotton balls
glue
black paper (head, wings)
yellow paper (feet, eyes)
orange paper (beak)
scissors

Directions:

Color the outside circle of the paper plate black. Glue the cotton balls evenly over the inside circle of the plate. Cut out a round head and wings from black paper. Cut out feet and eyes from yellow paper. Finally, cut out a beak from orange paper. Attach the penguin parts to the paper plate with glue.

Name _____

Directions: Complete the penguin poem by filling in the blanks with the correct rhyming words from the list below.

Five Penguins

This little penguin has little black feet.

He's a Blackfooted Penguin with feathers so _neat_.

This little penguin is called an Adélie.

On snow he can walk or slide on his _belly_.

This little penguin has more than one yellow feather.

He's a Macaroni Penguin. He likes cold kinds of _weather_.

These big penguins are known as Kings.

And although they can't fly, they can swim with their _wings_.

This big penguin is the biggest of all.

He's an Emperor Penguin, over three feet _tall_.

All penguins are birds, mostly black and white.

Any penguin you see is a beautiful _sight_.

Word List

weather	belly	neat
tall	sight	wings

King Penguin   **Blackfooted Penguin**   **Adélie Penguin**   **Macaroni Penguin**   **Emperor Penguin**

Design Your Own Flag of Antarctica

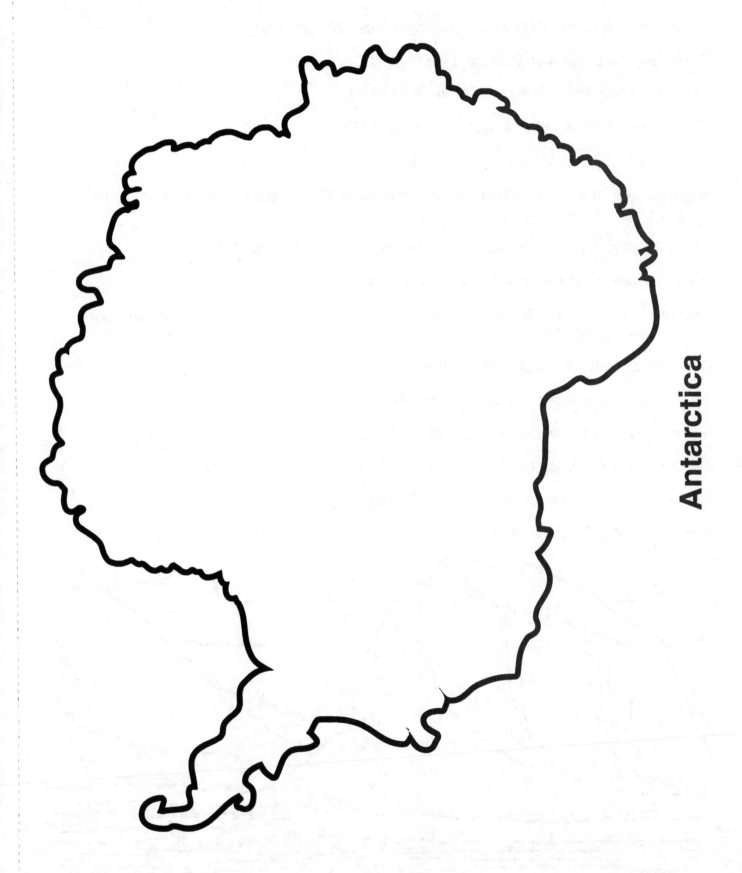

Antarctica

Teacher Resources

Asimov, Isaac. *How Did We Find Out About Antarctica?* Walker & Company, 1979.

Dewey, Jennifer 0. *Birds of Antarctica.* Little Brown & Co., 1989.

Fine, Jill. *The Shackleton Expedition.* Children's Press, 2002.

Glimmerveen, Ulco. *A Tale of Antarctica.* Scholastic, 1990.

Hackwell, John. *Desert of Ice.* Atheneum, 1991.

Hopper, Meredith and M.P. Robertson. *The Endurance: Shackleton's Perilous Expedition to Antarctica.* Abbeville Kids, 2001.

Icenhower, Joseph Bryan. *The First Book of the Antarctic.* Franklin Watts, 1971.

Lye, Keith. *Take a Trip to Antarctica.* Franklin Watts, 1984.

McCurdy, Michael. *Trapped by the Ice!: Shackleton's Amazing Antarctic Adventure.* Walker Books for Young Readers, 2002.

Osborne, Ben. *Antarctic Wildlife.* Mallard Press, 1989.

Peterson, David. *Antarctica.* Children's Press, 1999.

Shannon, Terry. *Antarctic Challenge.* Children's Press, 1973.

Steward, Gail B. *Antarctica.* Crestwood, 1991.

Stone, Lynn M. *Life in the Antarctic.* Rourke Publishing Group, 1995.

Winkler, Suzanne. *Our Endangered Planet, Antarctica.* Lerner Publications, 1992.

A Visit to South Africa

Area: 435,047 sq. miles
Capital Cities: Pretoria, Cape Town,
           and Bloemfontein
Population: 54,841,552
Main Language(s): Eleven official languages
           including Isizulu, IsiXhasa,
           Afrikaans, and English
Main Religion(s): Zion Christian,
           Pentecostal, and
           Methodist
Currency: Rand
Government: Republic
Flag:

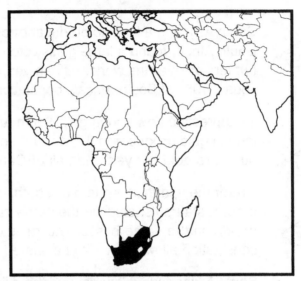

The flag of South Africa, adopted in 1994, includes the colors of all parties that took place in ending apartheid. Black, yellow, and green are the three colors of the major black parties. Red, white, and blue are the colors from the British and Dutch flags. The "Y" shape represents the union of the two sides into a unified entity.

For Your Information

The Republic of South Africa lies at the southern tip of the African continent. The Indian Ocean washes against South Africa's eastern shore and the South Atlantic Ocean forms the nation's western border.

The South African economy is the most diversified and developed in Africa, but tremendous differences exist between the economies of the homelands and white areas. There are important economic, social, and political differences between the racial groups. Until 1991, all development took place within the framework of **apartheid** ("apartness" in Afrikaans), a system of legalized racial separation that had been firmly enforced by the ruling white minority since 1948.

South African law recognizes four racial groups: native Africans, blacks (79% of the total population); whites (9.6%); mixed-race South Africans (8.9%); and Asians (2.5%). The whites form the second largest racial group and dominate South Africa's political and economic institutions. They comprise two main groups: Afrikaners (60%), who are descended from seventeenth-century Dutch settlers, and the English-speaking group (34%), who are descendants of British settlers who arrived as early as 1820.

The wildlife of South Africa is extremely rich. Elephants, rhinoceroses, giraffes, zebras, antelopes, and other wildlife are protected in such game reserves as Kruger National Park, Mkuze, and Hluhluwe. Bird life is varied, and more than 100 species of snakes are native to the area.

Fascinating Facts

 South Africa is a leading producer of diamonds and gold. In 1867, a boy from Kimberly, South Africa, found a large glassy stone. It was a diamond, and word spread to fortune hunters all over the world. Fifteen years later, gold was discovered near Johannesburg. Today, 40% of South Africa's population is employed in the gold mines.

 To appreciate how rich in gold South Africa is, one can compare it to Canada, the fourth largest gold producer in the world. There is one mine near Johannesburg that turns out more gold per year than all of Canada's mines combined!

 Under the apartheid system of South Africa, blacks and whites could not eat together in most restaurants, study in the same classroom, worship together in most churches, or ride on the same buses. The rules of apartheid have been abolished, and a new constitution allows power to be shared by blacks and whites.

 South Africans love sports, and the mild temperatures are perfect for outdoor recreation. Rugby football is the most popular sport in the winter, while cricket is enjoyed in the summer. Because of apartheid, the Olympic Games boycotted South Africa for dozens of years which drove many black and white athletes into exile. Two of the most well-known South-African athletes are the long distance runners Sidney Maree and Zola Budd.

 An upside-down tree? South Africa is home to the fascinating *baobab* tree. Early European settlers were stunned when they first saw the baobab trees, for they have a very interesting look. The trunks of the trees are so thick that in some cases their distance around exceeds their height. It also looks as though the baobab tree grows upside down with its roots, rather than its branches, spread in the air.

 In some rural places of South Africa, many species of wildlife still roam freely. Near the suburbs of Cape Town, wild baboons sometimes swarm atop slow-moving buses. Signs reading "DON'T FEED THE BABOONS" are as common in South Africa as signs in the United States that read "KEEP OFF THE GRASS."

 Although South Africa has a pleasantly warm climate, occasionally snow will fall in the higher regions. When snow does accumulate, an unusual practice occurs in the townships surrounding Johannesburg: instead of making snowmen, the black children make large deer out of the snow. No one can explain how, when, or why this custom began.

 The cities of South Africa are very "Americanized" and are kept quite spotless. Although shopping malls and movie theaters are common, the nation's cities have virtually no nightlife. Most restaurants, stores, and theaters close their doors at 9:00 p.m. City officials, who are usually conservative Afrikaners, disapprove of people entertaining into the evening hours. There is also the fear of common street crime.

40

Language Activities

Common Afrikaans Words

mammie	mom
pappie	dad
ouma	grandma
oupa	grandpa
ja	yes
nee	no
vriend	friend
skool	school
goeie môre	good morning
goeie naand	good evening
eina!	ouch!

Numbers

een	one
twee	two
drie	three
vier	four
vyf	five
ses	six
sewe	seven
ag	eight
nege	nine
tien	ten

Colors

rooi	red
oranje	orange
geel	yellow
groen	green
blou	blue
pers	pink

Days of the Week

Sondag	Sunday
Maandag	Monday
Dinsdag	Tuesday
Woensdag	Wednesday
Donderdag	Thursday
Vrydag	Friday
Saterdag	Saturday

Months of the Year

Januarie	January
Februarie	February
Maart	March
April	April
Mei	May
Junie	June
Julie	July
Augustus	August
September	September
Oktober	October
November	November
Desember	December

Jan Pierewiet
Afrikaans Poem

Jan Pierewiet, Jan Pierewiet
Jan Pierewiet, staan stil.
Jan Pierewiet, Jan Jan Pierewiet
Jan Jan Pierewiet, staan stil.

Goei more, my vrou,
Hier's 'n soentijie vir jou.
Goeie more, my man
Daar is koffie in die kan.

Jan Pierewiet, Jan Pierewiet
Jan Pierewiet, stand still.
Jan Pierewiet, Jan Pierewiet
Jan Pierewiet, stand still.

Good morning, my wife,
Here's a kiss for you.
Good morning, my husband
There's coffee in the pot.

South African Recipes

Vegetable Casserole of South Africa

Ingredients:
1¾ + ¼ sticks butter
2 large onions, chopped
2 cloves garlic, minced
6 zucchini, cut into chunks
6 yellow squash, cut into chunks
4 carrots, grated
2 teaspoons curry powder
½ teaspoon salt
¼ teaspoon pepper
2 cups plain yogurt
1½ cups unsalted sugar-free peanut butter
2 cups crushed dry herb stuffing

Directions:
Lightly grease a 4-quart casserole dish. In a large skillet, heat 1¾ sticks of butter. Add the onion and garlic, then cook until softened. Add the zucchini and squash, and cook for about two minutes. Add the carrots, curry powder, salt, and pepper and stir for about 1 minute. Set the skillet aside.

In a large bowl, mix yogurt and peanut butter. Add the vegetables and mix together. Transfer to a casserole dish and dot with remaining butter. Sprinkle herb stuffing on top. Bake at 350° for 30 minutes.

South African Apples and Cheese Crumble

Ingredients:
4 cups apples; peeled, cored, and sliced*
¼ cup lemon juice
1 cup sugar
¾ cup flour
½ teaspoon cinnamon
¼ teaspoon nutmeg
dash of salt
½ cup butter, softened
1½ cups grated cheddar cheese

Directions:
Mound apples in a 9" buttered pie plate. Sprinkle with lemon juice. Combine dry ingredients and cut in butter. Spread the mixture over apples. Top with cheese. Bake at 375° for 45 minutes. *(Use South African apples if they are available from a local grocer.)

There are three capitals of South Africa. The legislative branch of the government is located in Cape Town, the administrative branch is in Pretoria, and the judicial branch is in the city of Bloemfontein. If the United States were to separate its three branches of government to different cities, which cities would your students choose? Have your students work in groups to select three cities and explain why they chose those locations for the branches of government.

In addition to the baobab tree, South Africa is home to other interesting trees, such as the ironwood and the stinkwood. Using encyclopedias and other reference materials, have your students research these fascinating trees and describe what makes them unique. Compare the South African trees to those in your state or region.

School children in South Africa love to play outdoor games. A popular recreational activity is a game called **rounders.** Similar to American baseball, rounders is played with a round, flat bat and a tennis ball. Two teams take turns playing infield and outfield and "round" the bases when they hit the ball. Using a table tennis paddle and tennis ball, play rounders with your class during recess.

Another popular sport in South Africa is a game called **net ball** which is similar to American basketball. In net ball there are seven players on a team who guard a specific zone and try to shoot the ball into a basket. Try playing net ball with your class. Keep in mind that there are two major differences from American basketball: in net ball, the players may *not* dribble the ball, and in South Africa the sport is played only by girls.

Since apartheid was abolished in 1991, many changes are apparent in South Africa. Have your students research information on apartheid. How has it affected the lives of the people in South Africa, and what changes still need to be made?

Due to the diversity of cultures, many different greetings are used in South Africa. English greetings such as "Good Morning" and "Hello" are frequently heard. Mixed-race people and Afrikaners greet friends with "Goeie more" while the Zulus say "Sakubona" and the Xhosa greet with "Molo." Shaking hands is common among whites, while friends in some black groups greet with a triple handshake that involves interlocking the "little" fingers, clasping fists, and interlocking fingers again. Have your students make up a new handshake or greeting and share it with the class.

The Zulu tribe of South Africa decorate their homes with colorful, textured wall hangings. Brighten your classroom or bulletin board with textured coil art. Glue burlap onto an 8½" x 11" piece of cardboard and trim the edges. Using glue, make a coiled spiral on the burlap. Carefully place yarn (preferably in earth tones) over the glue coil. Repeat with different colors of yarn to make colorful abstract wall hangings.

Name _____

Directions: Fill in the boxes with writing or pictures to complete the newspaper "articles."

SOUTH AFRICAN NEWS

Date:

South African Athletes Win the Trophy

(sports)

Animal Escapes from Kruger National Park

(animals)

Zulu Dancers Perform at Festival

(cultures)

South Africans in the News

(people)

Miners Strike it Rich!

(products)

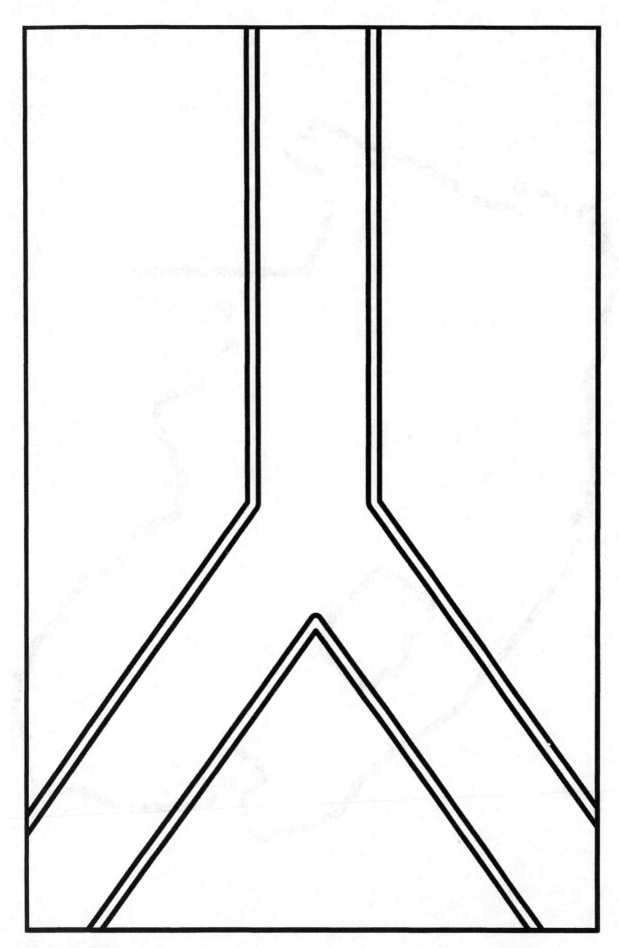

The Flag of South Africa

45

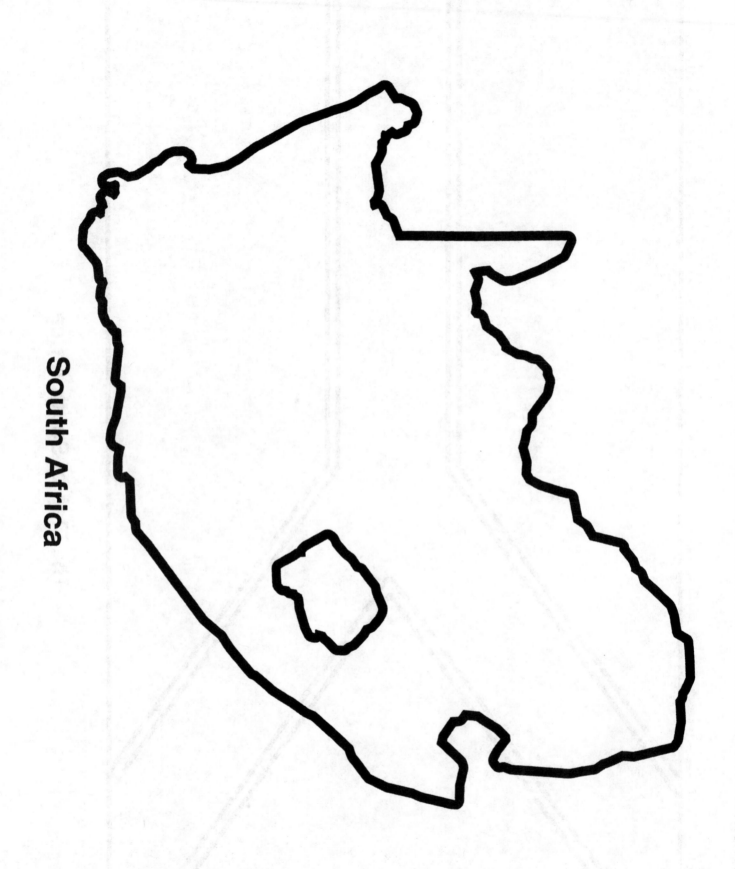

South Africa

Teacher Resources

Brickhill, Joan. *South Africa, the End of Apartheid?* Gloucester Press, 1991.

Canesso, Claudia and Beneke, Jeff. *South Africa.* Chelsea House, 1998.

Evans, Michael. *South Africa.* Franklin Watts, 1988.

Jacobsen, Karen. *South Africa* (A *New True Book*). Children's Press, 1991.

Heinrichs, Ann. *South Africa.* Children's Press, 1997.

Hoberman, Gerald and Marc. *South Africa.* Gerald and Marc Hoberman Collection, 2003.

Lawson, Don. *South Africa.* Franklin Watts, 1986.

Pascoe, Elaine. *South Africa, Troubled Land.* Franklin Watts, 1992.

Pogrund, Benjamin. *Nelson Mandela.* Blackbirch Press, 2003.

Rhythm of Resistance: Black Music of South Africa. Shnachie Records, 1988.

Rogers, Barbara R. *South Africa (Children of the World* Series). G. Stevens, 1991.

Rosmarin, Ike. *South Africa (Cultures of the World* Series). Benchmark Books, 2003.

Smith, Chris. *Conflict in South Africa.* New Discovery Books, 1993.

Stein, R. Conrad. *South Africa (Enchantment of the World* Series). Children's Press, 1989.

Watson, R. L. *South Africa in Pictures.* Lerner Publications, 1988.

Wepman, Dennis. *Desmond Tutu.* Franklin Watts, 1989.

Traveling to Nigeria

Area: 357,000 sq. miles
Capital City: Abuja
Population: 190,632,261
Main Language(s): English
Main Religion(s): Islam and Christianity
Currency: Naira
Government: Military
Flag:

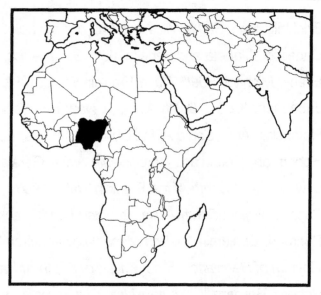

The flag of Nigeria was adopted in 1960. The two green stripes represent the agriculture of Nigeria while the white stripe in the middle symbolizes unity and peace.

For Your Information

The Federal Republic of Nigeria, located on the Atlantic coast in West Africa, is bordered by Benin on the west, Niger and Chad on the north, and Cameroon on the east. Nigeria has the largest population in Africa. Nigeria is a country of tremendous cultural and human diversities. Formerly a British colony, Nigeria gets its name from the Niger River.

About 250 different ethnic groups live in Nigeria. Four ethnic groups together account for about 68% of the total population: the Fulani, the Hausa, the Ibo, and the Yoruba. People in these ethnic groups may speak two or three languages. About 70 out of every 100 adults in Nigeria can read and write.

Nigeria is famous for its variety in art. The oldest known African sculptures are terra-cotta (clay) figures from 500 B.C., found in central Nigeria. Some of the finest wood carvings in Africa are found in Nigeria. Male wood carvers called **onishona** (people who make art), train for years to learn the art of wood carving. They carve masks and figures of gods and goddesses for shrines and festivals.

Nigeria has two seasons, a rainy season and a dry season. The length of the rainy season varies from nearly twelve months on the coast to less than five months inland. Parts of northern Nigeria may endure as long as five to seven months without rain. The average high temperature can be 101° to 105° in the dry months. Lake Chad, in northern Nigeria, is the shallowest lake of its size in the world. During the dry season, the lake may lose almost half of its size.

Yams are considered a staple part of the Nigerian diet, for they are grown in abundance in southern Nigeria. Cassava, rice, and plantains are also grown. In the northern part of Nigeria, millet, sorghum, peanuts, cotton, and rice are the leading crops.

Fascinating Facts

 Daily exchange of greetings and friendly interchange are an important aspect of life for Nigerians. No quick "hello" will do. Rather, one is expected to inquire about the health of family and friends and fellow workers followed by a cheerful hello such as *zaki,* a Kaleri greeting. Nigerians are also very hospitable. Strangers are greeted with great respect and, in most cases, offered food and lodging.

 Nigerians love music and it has always been important to the people and their culture. In addition to singing and dancing, drums are popular instruments as well as raft zithers, thumb pianos, and metal gongs. Musicians also play a stringed instrument called the *molo,* which has three or four strings, and a reed flute called the *algaita.*

 There are at least 250 languages or ethnic groups in Nigeria and more than 400 languages or dialects are spoken. The Yoruba people speak a tonal language which means that the same combination of sounds may have different meanings depending on the tone used in pronunciation.

 A very important family custom is the *naming ceremony.* Seven days after the birth of a child, the new father gives kola nuts to family and friends. This signifies an invitation to join the celebration and praise the newborn. The kola nut is chewed as a kind of stimulant. Another treat is *halawa*, a kind of sugar candy pulled like taffy.

 Nigeria has extremely rich traditions connected with early religious beliefs, rites, and practices. All tribes have their own religious rituals, and about 10% of the people observe the traditional African religions worshipping many gods and spirits.

 Traditionally, marriages in Nigeria have been polygamous (one husband, many wives). Marriage customs differ among ethnic groups, but most require that a *bride price* be paid by the prospective groom. In polygamous marriages, the first wife is usually the leader among the wives. The man is the head of the household, and the wives usually do what their husbands ask. The wives, however, are in control of the kitchen. If the husband wants more food and the wives say no, he will not argue with them.

 Throughout Nigeria, men in nearly every ethnic group observe the custom of the *special friend.* These friendships begin in boyhood and last throughout life. The special friends are often allowed into areas of the house reserved for family, and men usually feel closer to their special friends than they do to their own families.

 Public markets are very important in Nigeria, and they are all organized and run by women. Goods such as fruits and vegetables, clay pots, cloth, and animals are often sold. In the city of Lagos, an entire section of the market is devoted to the selling of *jujus* (the charms, potions, herbs, and other items still believed by many to have magical powers).

Language Activities

Nigerian Folktales

Although English is the national language of Nigeria, Hausa is the dominant language in the northern part of the country. From the Hausa people comes a famous set of folktales that tell of a spider named Anansi. Here is a story about Anansi that explains why spiders live in webs. *

A monkey and a tiger were chasing Anansi, so he asked a banana tree for help. The tree gave Anansi one of its many strong fibers. The spider took the fiber and climbed a nearby tree. He tied the fiber to two branches and held onto the fiber.

The monkey and tiger waited for Anansi to get hungry and come down out of the tree. Soon Anansi grew very hungry. He knew that if he climbed down from the tree that the monkey and tiger would catch him.

He decided to stay in the tree and find food. Anansi added many threads to his fiber, and soon a fly was caught in the web he had created.

Today the spider still lives in a web to catch its food.

*Based on a story from *Anansi: The Spider Man* by Philip Sherlock (Thomas Crowell Co., NY, 1954)

The Yoruba, another major Nigerian group, have many creation stories. One of these tales tells how the land on earth was formed. *

Odudwa, one of the gods, gathered together some sand, some chameleons, some chickens, and many chains. The most powerful of all the gods tied Odudwa to heaven by the chains and then lowered him down towards earth.

There was no land onto which Odudwa could set foot, so he poured some sand into the sea.

First, the chameleons walked very carefully across the new land, one step at a time. Next, the chickens all landed safely. Finally, Odudwa released himself from the chains and went to live on the earth he had formed.

Eventually, all the other gods from heaven joined Odudwa, and he became the most powerful of all the gods as a result of his bravery.

* Based on a story from *Cultures of the World: Nigeria* by Patricia Levy (Marshall Cavendish, 1993)

Nigerian Recipes

Fu Fu

Ingredients (Quantities vary. Experiment, and judge for yourself.):
water
farina (buckwheat or another coarse flour)
cooked yams, mashed
biscuit mix

Directions:
Bring the water to a boil, then add farina, yams, and biscuit mix. Add enough of all the ingredients to create a thick consistency. As the mixture begins to thicken, stir vigorously until it is very stiff. Scoop the mixture onto a large plate and serve it with soup.

Banana Fritters

Ingredients:
2½ cups flour
 ½ cup sugar
 2 teaspoons cinnamon
 2 eggs
 1 cup milk
 6 bananas, mashed
   oil
   confectioner's sugar

Directions:
In a large bowl, combine flour, sugar, and cinnamon. Beat in eggs. Gradually add the milk and continue to beat until the batter is smooth. Stir in bananas. Pour batter by scant ¼ cupfuls onto hot griddle. Cook 2-3 minutes on each side. Sprinkle with confectioner's sugar just before serving.

Pottery of all sizes is a popular craft of Nigerian women. Clay pots are often used for storing water or as musical instruments. Let your students make their own pots out of clay (found at craft stores). Decorate the outside with African designs. When the pots are dry, the students can write a story about a magical Nigerian pot.

Nigerian children rarely play with manufactured toys. Instead, they frequently play outdoor games such as soccer, hide-and-seek, **tuu-ma-tu** (hopscotch), marbles, and a jumping game called **ampe.** Have your children write about their favorite outdoor games to play. Would their playtime activities change drastically if they didn't have their manufactured toys? If they could share a toy or game with a Nigerian child, what would it be?

The open-air markets are very important in Nigeria. Women sell a variety of goods there as well as greet friends and bargain on prices. Have your students conduct their own open-air market on the playground. Each child can make an item to sell and students can barter for different items using play money.

Although Lagos, Nigeria, is the third largest city in Africa and is becoming quite "westernized," many Nigerians live in rural villages without many modern conveniences. Have your students create a bulletin board that compares the lifestyles of people living in the cities of Nigeria to those living in small villages. How does living in Nigeria compare to living in the United States? What are some similarities and differences?

In the rural villages of southern Nigeria, people live in homes made from **pisa** clay. The mud walls and thatched roofs are just right for Nigeria's hot climate. In the daytime, the pisa walls keep out the hot sunshine. At night, the mud bricks release the heat they have absorbed during the day and warm the inside of the house. Have your students make a village of pisa houses. Cut a plastic 2-liter soda bottle in half for each child. Recycle the lower halves of the bottles. Have children cover their bottles with masking tape, paint over the tape with orange or brown tempera paint, then glue straw or hay on the tops of the bottles for the roofs.

52

Art Activities

Nigerian lya llu Drum

Drums are an important instrument in Nigeria. In addition to providing rhythm for dances, the lya ilu or **talking drums** are used to send messages.

Materials:
small terra-cotta flowerpot
markers or paint
paper grocery bag
paper tape (the type moistened with water)

Directions:
Using colorful markers or paint, decorate the outside of the flowerpot and let dry. Cut a circle from the paper bag about 3" larger than the open end of the flowerpot. Dampen the circle and lay it over the open end. Pull the bag tight and tape it in place. Wrap tape around the top several times. When the paper is dry, your drum is ready to be played! Rat-a-tat-tat!

African Beads

Nigerians love to dress up and look beautiful. Beads are an important part of their cultural heritage. The designs, patterns and colors of the beads indicate a Nigerian's position in his society and religion. Beads are often worn around the head, neck, ears, and ankles.

Materials:
4 cups flour
2 cups salt
2 cups water
large bowl
baking tray
toothpicks
acrylic paints
shellac
string

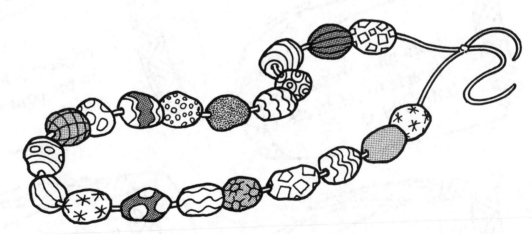

Directions:
Mix together the flour and salt. Gradually add the water and knead the dough until thoroughly mixed and smooth. Form small beads out of the dough about ½" to 1" thick. Fifteen to twenty beads will be needed for each necklace. Push a toothpick through the center of each bead to make a hole. Bake for 15 to 20 minutes in a 350° oven (check oven frequently). When completely cool, decorate the beads with paint and let dry. Shellac the beads and dry overnight. String the beads on a 24-inch length of string.

Name _____

Directions: Read the sentence inside each drum. If the statement is **true,** color the drum **green.** If the statement is **false,** color the drum **orange.**

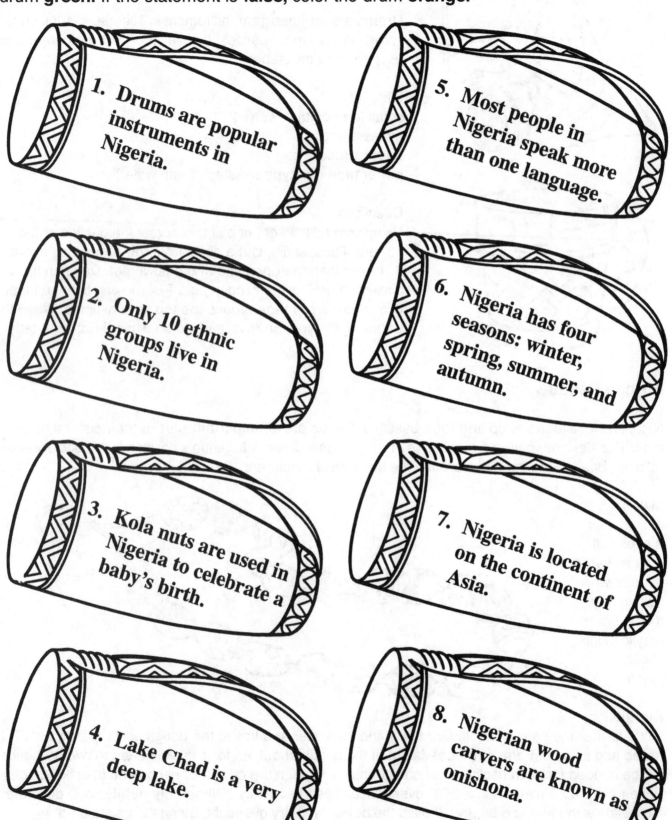

1. Drums are popular instruments in Nigeria.

2. Only 10 ethnic groups live in Nigeria.

3. Kola nuts are used in Nigeria to celebrate a baby's birth.

4. Lake Chad is a very deep lake.

5. Most people in Nigeria speak more than one language.

6. Nigeria has four seasons: winter, spring, summer, and autumn.

7. Nigeria is located on the continent of Asia.

8. Nigerian wood carvers are known as onishona.

The Flag of Nigeria

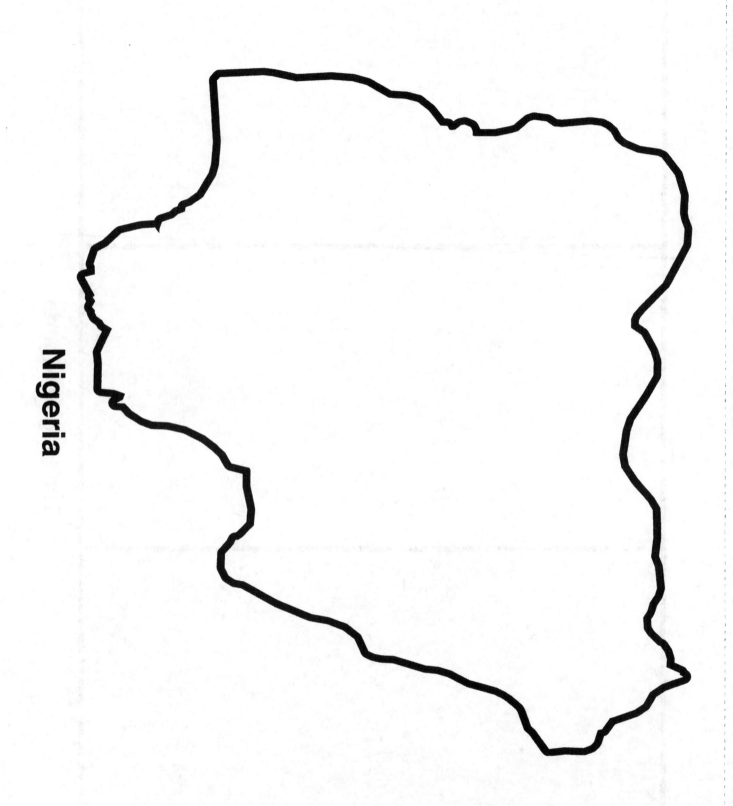

Nigeria

Teacher Resources

Aardema, Verna. *Bringing the Rain to Kapiti Plain.* Puffin, 1992.

Aardema, Verna. *Why Mosquitoes Buzz in People's Ears: A West African Tale.* Puffin, 1992.

Anderson, Lydia. *Nigeria, Cameroon and the Central African Republic.* Franklin Watts, 1981.

Barker, Carol. *A Family in Nigeria.* Lerner Pub. Group, 1985.

Echewa, T. Obinkaram. *The Ancestor Tree.* Dutton Juvenile Books, 1994.

Emecheta, Buchi. *The Moonlight Bride.* G. Braziller, 1983.

Emecheta, Buchi. *The Wrestling Match.* G. Braziller, 1983.

Gerson, Mary-Joan. *Omoteji's Baby Brother.* Random House, 1974.

Haliburton, Warren. *Celebrations of African Heritage.* Crestwood House, 1992.

Hamilton, Janice. *Nigeria in Pictures.* Lerner Publications, 2003.

Jacobsen, Peter Otto. *A Family in West Africa.* Bookwrights Press, 1985.

Jenness, Alyette. *Along the Niger River: An African Way of Life.* Ty Crowell Company, 1974.

Knight, Margy Burns. *Africa Is Not a Country.* Millbrook Press, 2002.

Lye, Keith. *Take a Trip to Nigeria.* Franklin Watts, 1984.

Nabwire, Constance. *Cooking the African Way.* Lerner Publishing Group, 1988.

Nicholas, Freville. *Nigeria (Let's Visit Series).* Chelsea House Pub., 1991.

Olaleye, Isaac. *The Distant Talking Drum.* Boyds Mill Press, 2001.

Onyefulu, Ifeoma. *A Is for Africa.* Cobblehill Books, 1993.

Rupert, Janet E. *The African Mask.* Clarion Books, 1994.

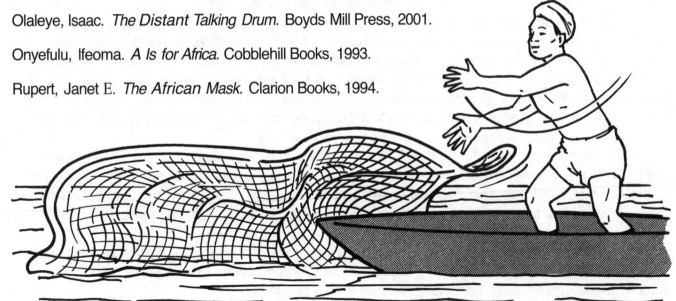

Landing in Israel

Area: 8,019 sq. miles
Capital City: Jerusalem
Population: 8,299,706
Main Language(s): Hebrew and Arabic
Main Religion(s): Judaism, Islam, and
Christianity
Currency: Shekel
Government: Parliamentary democracy
Flag:

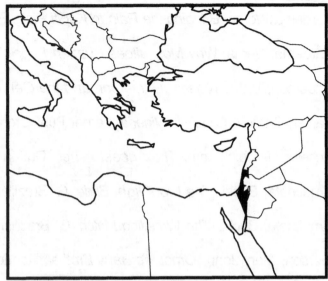

Israel's flag is white with a blue hexagram (six-pointed linear star) known as the Star of David. The Star is centered between two equal horizontal blue bands near the top and bottom of the flag .

For Your Information

Israel, a small, independent nation in southwest Asia, is located on the eastern shore of the Mediterranean Sea. On May 14, 1948, Israel was established as a Jewish state on land that had been part of the British mandate for Palestine. Historically, it is considered the Holy Land for Jews, Christians, and Muslims. Most of the people of Israel are Jews, about half of whom were born in other countries. Israel makes up most of the region once called Palestine, the Holy Land of the Bible. Even Jews who live elsewhere consider Israel their spiritual home.

Centuries ago, the Jews of Palestine were forced to leave their homeland and live in other areas of the world. The new Israel was formed after World War II in 1948. It had about 806,000 people living there. Today, Israel's population, although unevenly distributed, is about 6 1/4 million. The area along the Mediterranean coast is Israel's most densely populated region. About 80% of Israel's people are Jews who share a common spiritual and historical heritage. Because they come from many countries, Israel's Jews belong to a number of different ethnic groups, each with its own cultural, political, and recent historical background.

Arabs make up nearly all of the remaining 20% of the population of Israel. Most of them are Palestinians whose families remained in Israel after the 1948-1949 Arab-Israeli War. Many live in their own farm villages or in the Arab neighborhoods of Israeli cities. Arab and Jewish Israelis have limited contact, in part because of their political disagreements, military conflicts, and other disputes.

Education is given a high priority in Israel. One of the first laws passed in Israel established free education and required school attendance for all children between the ages of 5 and 14. School attendance today is mandatory and free from age 6 to 18.

Fascinating Facts

 Israel is the only country that contains the major holy places of the Jewish and Christian religions and the third holiest site of the Muslim religion. Jerusalem is considered the holiest of all cities. No other city in the world is so important to such a great number of people with such different beliefs.

 Float all day! In Israel's Dead Sea, the waters of the lake are two percent salt, three times as salty as ocean water. The water is so thick with salt and minerals that everything and everyone, even a nonswimmer, floats on the surface. The land around the Dead Sea is the lowest point on earth, 1,296 feet below sea level.

 A favorite pastime of Israelis is reading. On average, more books are read and published in Israel than in any other country in the world. Israel also has more newspapers per capita than any other country. There are a total of 30 different daily newspapers.

 Watching television is not free in Israel. Viewers have to pay a license fee. One of the favorite children's TV shows is called **Rehov Sum-Sum** or "Sesame Street." However, instead of Big Bird, the main character is a big-hearted porcupine called Kippy. Arik and Benz are Ernie and Bert, and the Cookie Monster is named Oogie because the Hebrew word for "cookie" is **oogiyah!**

 Basketball and soccer are very popular sports in Israel, and occasionally the fans can become quite excited. They shout, boo, stamp their feet, and devour tons of popcorn and ice cream. One soccer team was penalized and not allowed to have home games for two months because its fans threw food at the opposing team.

 Every four years since 1932, Israel has hosted the Maccabiah Games, patterned after the Olympics for Jewish athletes. Jewish sports champions from all over the world compete against each other. Many American Jewish athletes, such as the swimmer Mark Spitz, earned their first medals at Israel's Maccabiah Games before going on to win gold, silver, and bronze medals at the Olympic Games.

 A favorite place for children to visit in Israel is the Biblical Zoo in Jerusalem. Here one can find every living creature that is mentioned in the Bible.

 Israelis also love going to movies. When the soundtrack is in English, however, the audience often gets so noisy one cannot hear a word. The patrons are not listening to the film; they are reading the Hebrew subtitles.

 In December, Jewish families celebrate Hanukkah in memory of the defeat of the Syrians by the Maccabees. The "Festival of Lights" holiday is full of songs, games, stories, and presents. Jewish people around the world celebrate Hanukkah by lighting one candle each of the eight nights of Hanukkah until all are lit on the last day of the holiday.

Language Activities

The Hebrew language is written from right to left. Hebrew has no capital letters and is printed without vowels, except in books written for children.

Hebrew Alphabet

Letter	Translation	Pronunciation
א	aleph	a (as in alpha)
ב	bet	b (as in boy)
ג	gimel	g (as in go)
ד	dalet	d (as in dog)
ה	heh	h (as in hear)
ו	vav	v (as in vest)
ז	zayin	z (as in zebra)
ח	het	h (glottal "h")
ט	tet	t (as in toe)
י	youd	y (as in yard)
כ	kaf	k (as in can)
ל	lamed	l (as in long)
מ	mem	m (as in mom)
נ	nun	n (as in no)
ס	samech	s (as in sorry)
ע	ayin	a (as in able)
פ	peh	p (as in pie)
צ	tzadi	tz (as in tse-tse fly)
ק	kuf	k (as in kick)
ר	resh	r (as in ring)
ש	shin	sh (as in shoe)
ת	taf	t (as in toe)

Hebrew Numbers

א	1	אחת ah-hat	one
ב	2	שתים shtah-yim	two
ג	3	שלש shah-losh	three
ד	4	חמש ar-bah	four
ה	5	חמש hay-mesh	five
ו	6	שש shesh	six
ז	7	שבע she-vah	seven
ח	8	שמונה shmoh-neh	eight
ט	9	תשע tay-shah	nine
י	10	עשר e-sair	ten

English Words Borrowed from Hebrew

English	Hebrew	Meaning
amen	amen	("truth")
camel	gamel	("camel")
cinnamon	kinnamon	(a spice)
hallelujah	hallelujah	("praise God")
lemon	limon	("lemon")
paradise	pardes	("orchard")
sack	sok	("bag")
sapphire	sapir	("precious stone")
sofa	sapa	("couch")
tunic	kutonet	("shirt")

Hebrew Names for Boys and Girls

Boys' Names		Boys' Names		Girls' Names		Girls' Names	
Ari	lion	**Gur**	lion cub	**Amira**	princess	**Shira**	song
Dan	judge	**Ilan**	tree	**Arella**	angel	**Sigal**	violet
Eyal	strength	**Sagi**	great	**Nitza**	blossom	**Vara**	rose
Gad	fortune	**Uri**	my light	**Noga**	brightness	**Yardena**	river
Gil	joy	**Zahi**	pure	**Orli**	my light	**Yifat**	beauty

Israeli Recipes

Hummus

Ingredients:

2 cups canned chick-peas, drained
juice of 2 lemons
1 teaspoon salt
¼ teaspoon cumin

3 tablespoons tahini paste
2 garlic cloves, mashed
2 tablespoons oil
pita bread, crackers

Directions:

Place all ingredients, except the pita bread and crackers, in a food processor or blender. Mix until smooth. Refrigerate several hours. Serve with pita bread or crackers.

Falafel (Israeli hamburger)

Falafel is sold on street corners in every city and town in Israel.

Ingredients:

1 lb. canned chick-peas, drained
1 large onion, chopped
2 tablespoons parsley, finely chopped
1 egg, lightly beaten
1 teaspoon salt

1 teaspoon garlic powder
1 teaspoon cumin
¾ cup bread crumbs
vegetable oil (for frying)

Directions:

Combine chick-peas with onion. Add parsley, egg, and spices. Mix in blender. Add bread crumbs until mixture forms a ball without sticking to your hands. Form small balls (about 1" in diameter) and flatten them slightly. Fry on both sides until golden brown. Serve individually with toothpicks.

Rugelach Pastries

Ingredients:
  Dough:
    2 oz. fresh yeast
    ½ cup lukewarm water
    1 teaspoon + ¾ cup sugar
    5 cups flour
    2 sticks margarine
    2 cups milk
    3 eggs, beaten
  Filling:
    jam
    mixture of 1 cup sugar and ⅓ cup cocoa

Directions:
Mix yeast with water and 1 teaspoon of sugar until yeast starts bubbling. Mix in the rest of the ingredients and knead until the dough does not stick to the bowl. Cool the dough in the refrigerator for 2 hours. Roll dough onto a clean, flat surface. Spread jam on dough, then top with the sugar and cocoa mixture. Cut into a triangle and place on a cookie sheet. Bake at 375° for 30 minutes.

Classroom Activities

About 6% of Israelis live on **a *kibbutz*** (a communal settlement where everything is shared on an equal basis). In these collective farms, everything is owned and decided by the community as a group. Adults share their jobs, wages, and tools. Children share their toys, clothes, bicycles, and even their food. Working in groups of 4-5 children, have your students set up their own classroom kibbutz for a day. Everything must be shared and children must work cooperatively on all of their daily tasks.

Israel is the only country that uses the Hebrew word for "peace," ***Shalom,*** as a daily greeting, even though the country has been at war for much of its short life. Have your students design a peace banner. Let them develop a phrase or slogan that will encourage different countries to live together in peace and harmony.

Many Jewish people follow ***kashrut***, or kosher, dietary laws. These laws specify acceptable and unacceptable foods. For example, they prohibit eating meat and dairy products at the same time. Pork and shellfish can never be eaten. Two sets of dishes, one for milk and the other for meat products, are used, stored, and cleaned separately. Invite a local rabbi (or another Jewish person) who follows these dietary laws to your classroom to teach your students more about kosher foods.

Rosh Hashanah, in September, is the Jewish New Year. It is the beginning of the High Holy Days and ends with Yom Kippur, the holiest day of the year. During this time Jewish people reflect on the past year. They ask forgiveness for their sins and pray that they will live well in the New Year. Have your students look back on their own past year. What are some accomplishments they are proud of? What are some things they did last year that they wish they had not done? Students can share their reflections with the class or take them home to their families.

Using the language activities on page 60, have your students adopt a Hebrew name for the day. Use a baby naming book to discover the origin of the names and to see if they have special meanings. The Hebrew numbers can be used to make a paper clock or for simple math problems. Let your students practice writing the Hebrew way, from right to left.

Children in Israel love to play games. A popular game played in the schoolyard is called ***Adras,*** an Israeli tic-tac-toe. Have students work with a partner to play this familiar game with a new twist.

Draw a diagram like the one pictured. Each player has three stones or markers. The players take turns placing their stones on one of the nine intersections. One stone is used for each move. The winner is the first player to get three stones in a line in any direction.

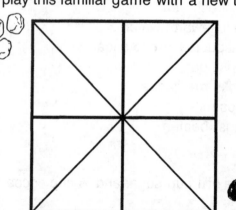

Art Activities

Hanukkah Dreidel

Jewish children enjoy playing with a **dreidel** (a square-sided top) during Hanukkah.

Materials:
2" square piece of cardboard
pencil
marker
gelt (tokens)

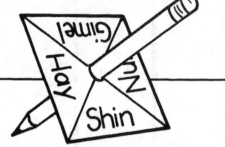

Directions:

Draw lines diagonally from corner to corner on the cardboard square, creating four triangular sections. In each section write one of the words **Nun** (none), **Gimel** (all), **Hay** (half), and **Shin** (add to). These are the first letters of **Nes gada/haya sham,** which means, "A great miracle happened here." Poke a small hole in the center of the cardboard and insert the pencil.

How to Play:

Each player places two gelt in the pot to begin the game. Players take turns spinning the dreidel and doing whatever is indicated by the letter it lands on. For example, if a player lands on **Shin,** he or she must add one token to the pot. If the dreidel lands on **Nun,** nothing is taken from the pot. If **Hay** comes up, that player receives half of the pot. If the dreidel lands on **Gimel,** he or she takes all of the gelt, and each player puts two back into the pot. The winner is the player who gets all of the gelt.

Star Chain

Materials:
rectangular sheets of paper (white and colored)
scissors

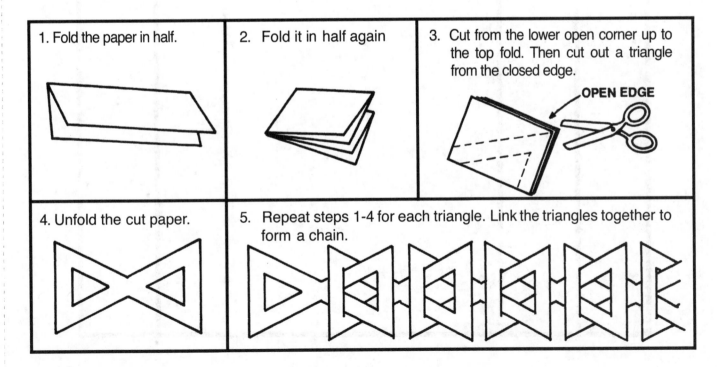

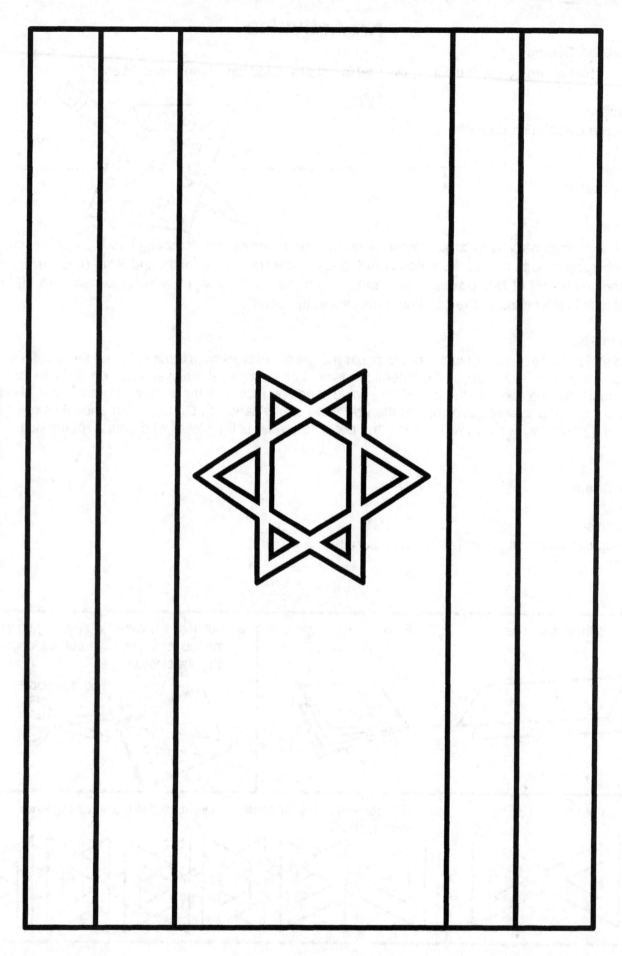

The Flag of Israel

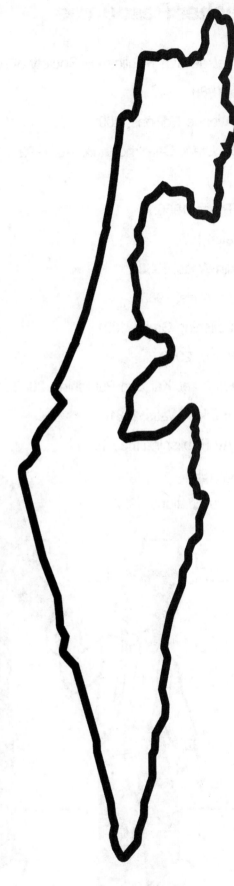

Israel

65

Teacher Resources

Burstein, Chaya M. *A Kid's Catalog of Israel.* Jewish Publication Society of America, 1998.

Cahill, Mary Jane. *Israel.* Chelsea House, 1988.

Grossman, Laurie. *Colors of Israel.* First Avenue Editions, 2001.

Haskins, James. *Count Your Way Through Israel.* Carolrhoda Books, 1992.

James, Ian. *Israel.* Franklin Watts, 1990.

Jones, Helen Hinckley. *Israel.* Children's Press, 1986.

Kubie, Nora Benjamin. *Israel.* Franklin Watts, 1978.

Lawton, Clive A. *Passport to Israel.* Franklin Watts, 1988.

Levine, Gemma. *We Live in Israel.* Franklin Watts, 1983.

Loewen, Nancy, *Food in Israel.* Rourke Publishing Group, 1991.

Rivlin, Lilly. *Welcome to Israel!* Behrman House, 2000.

Rouss, Sylvia A. *Sammy Spider's First Trip to Israel.* Kar-Ben Publishing, 2002.

Rutland, Jonathan. *Take a Trip to Israel.* Franklin Watts, 1981.

Scharfstein, Sol. *Understanding Israel.* KTAV Publishing Inc., 1994.

Smith, Debbie. *Israel: The Land.* Crabtree, 1998.

Taylor, Allegra. *A Kibbutz in Israel.* Lerner Publications, 1987.

Touring Greece

Area: 50,962 sq. miles
Capital City: Athens
Population: 10,768,477
Main Language(s): Greek
Main Religion(s): Greek Orthodox Church
Currency: Euro
Government: Republic
Flag:

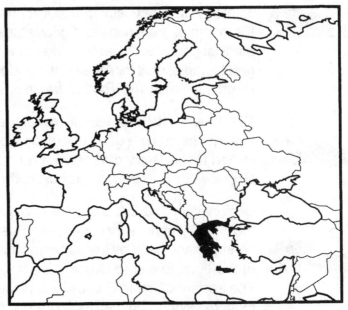

Adopted in 1822, the Greek flag has a white cross in the upper left-hand corner symbolizing the Greek Orthodox religion. The flag's blue stripes represent the sea and sky. The white stripes stand for the purity of the struggle for independence.

For Your Information

Greece, where Western civilization started about 2,500 years ago, is a mountainous country with more than 400 islands providing the most spectacular setting in the Mediterranean Sea. Although Greece is about the size of Florida, it has more miles of coastline than the entire continental United States.

Greece is predominantly an agricultural country, although less than one-third of its area is cultivated. The country is self-sufficient in basic foods, and agricultural products make up most of Greece's exports. Tourism accounts for an important part of Greece's national income.

Athens, one of the world's most historic cities, is the capital and the largest city of Greece. In Athens, as well as other parts of Greece, magnificent ruins stand as monuments to the nation's glorious past. The Acropolis, the center of ancient Athens, is the most famous attraction. The Acropolis includes the beautiful ruins of the Parthenon and several temples standing on this rocky hilltop.

About 98 percent of Greece's people belong to the Greek Orthodox Church. Most Greeks attend church during such events as baptisms, weddings, and funerals, and during the major religious holidays of Easter and Christmas. As a sign of respect for the dead, many Greeks wear black all of the time, not just during periods of mourning.

Greeks enjoy sports, particularly soccer and swimming. They also enjoy socializing in outdoor theatres, cafes, and restaurants. On weekends and holidays, Greeks like to travel to visit with friends and relatives in other parts of the country .

Fascinating Facts

To many ancient Greeks, Mt. Olympus, the highest point in Greece, was believed to be the home of great gods and goddesses. The Greeks believed in and worshipped these magical gods, for it was their way of explaining the world around them. In 438 B.C., a great temple, built for Athena, the goddess of war, was completed on top of the Acropolis in Athens. Today, the **Parthenon** is one of the most popular tourist attractions in Greece.

Greeks are extremely friendly people, especially to strangers. Ancient Greeks thought a stranger might be a god in disguise, so they were kind to everyone. Strangers are often invited to the family dinner even after a chance conversation on the street. In fact, the Greek word for "strange," **xenos,** is the same as the word for "guest."

Beginning in 776 B.C., athletes and spectators from all over Greece would travel to the town of Olympia every four years to participate in the Olympic Games. The games were so important that the Greeks temporarily halted any wars that might have been going on at the time. Even the Greek calendar was based on the game's beginning and ending. The ancient Olympic Games took place every four years for 1,170 years. In 1896, the first modern Olympic Games took place in Athens.

Greeks love crowds. Many dislike solitude and do not consider a vacation to be a chance to "get away from it all." Rather, at the seashore, most families will seek out the most crowded beaches to spread their blankets. The word for "private" in the Greek language is **idiotikos,** the root word for "idiot."

Due to government control, many Greeks feel that the quality of movies and television programs is poor. On the other hand, Greece is alive with theater productions. The demand for theater space is so great that stages are often built in garages, warehouses, and abandoned factory buildings. Dramatic plays are still held in open-air theaters built more than 2,000 years ago.

Many restaurants in Greece, called **tavernas**, serve their food lukewarm. This often frustrates tourists, but the Greeks claim the cooler temperature brings out the flavor. Service at restaurants often begins at 9:00 p.m., and dinners can be ordered well after midnight. When dining, Greeks keep their wrists on the table at all times, never in their laps.

Birthdays are not always celebrated in Greece. Instead, boys and girls celebrate their "name day," honoring the patron saint after which they were named. For example, on St. Andrew's Day, everyone named Andrew celebrates his name day by having a party. Guests will often greet the honored child with the two-word greeting, "Many years."

Traffic in the capital, Athens, is horrendous. It is usually faster to walk than to take a taxi. However, pedestrians must be extremely careful when crossing the city streets because many drivers will simply ignore the traffic lights. Some city planners would like to ban all private automobiles from Athens.

Language Activities

Greek Alphabet

Letter		Translation	Pronunciation	Letter		Translation	Pronunciation
A	α	alpha	(*a* as in *a*rm)	N	ν	nu	(*n* as in *n*urse)
B	β	beta	(*b* as in *b*oy)	Ξ	ξ	xi	(*x* as in bo*x*)
Γ	γ	gamma	(*g* as in *g*o)	O	o	omicron	(*o* as in *o*r)
Δ	δ	delta	(*d* as in *d*og)	Π	π	pi	(*p* as in *p*ie)
E	ε	epsilon	(*e* as in t*e*n)	P	ρ	rho	(*r* as in *r*ed)
Z	ζ	zeta	(*z* as in *z*oo)	Σ	σ	sigma	(*s* as in *s*it)
H	η	eta	(*ee* as in t*ee*th)	T	τ	tau	(*t* as in *t*ake)
Θ	θ	theta	(*th* as in *th*ick)	Y	υ	upsilon	(*ee* as in t*ee*th)
I	ι	iota	(*ee* as in t*ee*th)	Φ	φ	phi	(*f* as in *f*unny)
K	κ	kappa	(*k* as in *k*ing)	X	χ	chi	(*x* or *ch* as in a*ch*e)
Λ	λ	lambda	(*l* as in *l*amp)	Ψ	ψ	psi	(*ps* as in li*ps*)
M	μ	mu	(*m* as in *m*an)	Ω	ω	omega	(*oh* as in l*ow*)

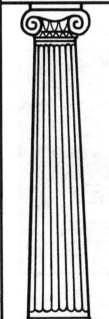

Everyday Greek Expressions

Χαίρετε	HEH-re-teh	Hello.
Γεία σου	YA-soo	Good-bye.
Καγημέρα	kah-lee-MEH-rah	Good morning.
παρακαγῶ	pah-rah-kah-LOH	please
Εύχαριστῶ	eff-hah-rees-TOH	Thank you.
Παρακαγῶ	pah-kah-kah-TOH	You're welcome.
Πῶζ είστε	poss eess-teh	How are you?
ταί	NEH	yes
όζι	OH-hee	no

Greek Recipes

Kourabiethes (Greek Butter Cookies)

Butter cookies are very popular in Greece. During the Christmas season, Greek women top their Kourabiethes with whole cloves to symbolize the spices brought by the three wise men.

Ingredients:
2½ cups flour
  1 teaspoon baking powder
  1 cup butter, softened
  ½ cup sugar
  1 egg
  ½ teaspoon vanilla extract
  ¼ teaspoon almond extract
    whole cloves
    powdered sugar (for sprinkling)

Directions: Combine flour and baking powder in a small bowl. Set aside. In a large bowl, beat together butter, sugar, and egg until light and fluffy. Add flour mixture and mix until well blended. Add vanilla and almond extracts. Mix well. With your hands, form dough (about ½ tablespoon at a time) into crescent shapes. Press cloves into the center of each cookie. Bake for 15 minutes in a 350° oven or until barely brown around the edges. Cool on wire rack and sprinkle with powdered sugar. Remove cloves before eating cookies.

Horiatiki Salata (Greek Country Salad)

This light and tasty salad is often served on warm evenings in Greek homes and tavernas.

Ingredients:
  4 tomatoes, cut into wedges
  1 cucumber, peeled and sliced
  1 green pepper, sliced in thin rings
  1 yellow or red pepper, sliced in thin rings
  1 mild onion, chopped
    salt and pepper
  4 tablespoons olive oil
  5 oz. feta cheese, crumbled
15 or more black olives
  1 small bunch of parsley, coarsely chopped
  1 teaspoon dried oregano

Directions: Place vegetables in a bowl, then sprinkle them with salt, pepper, and olive oil. Toss well. Arrange the feta cheese, olives, and herbs on top.

Classroom Activities

Many students in your class may already be familiar with *Aesop's Fables.* Aesop was believed to be a Greek slave who was famed as a teller of fables around 600 B.C. Each of his fables ended with a brief lesson or moral. Read to your class some of Aesop's more popular fables, such as "Lion and the Mouse," "Tortoise and the Hare," or ''Town Mouse and Country Mouse.'' Students can work with partners to decide the moral or write fables of their own.

When frustrated or tense, many Greeks will twirl a string of beads called **komboloi** or "worry beads." Kombologia beads are sold in stores throughout Greece. Greek students may swing their beads before an exam, and in heavy traffic, drivers may fondle them to relieve tension. Have your students string a variety of beads on a 24-inch length of string. Students can then write about the different times that they may need their komboloi or worry beads.

Set up an Olympic day in your classroom. Let students work in cooperative groups to brainstorm different Olympic sports or add new sports to the Olympic list. Your students can then choose a sport in which they would like to compete. Students can design gold, silver, and bronze medals to be awarded (make enough so that each child will receive a medal). During the awards ceremony, you may want to play a recording of "Fanfare for the Common Man," by Aaron Copland, or the "Star Spangled Banner." For a different kind of Olympics, hold an Academic Olympics and give medals for the best speller, timed math tests, etc.

Socrates, an ancient Greek philosopher, felt ignorance is the cause of all evil and that knowledge is acquired through asking questions. Have your students write a variety of questions they would like to be answered. The questions can be answered by the teacher or traded among classmates to be taken home and answered for homework. Students can also interview older students and adults for questions that they may have.

Share with your class some tales from Greek mythology. Your students may be particularly interested in the following gods and goddesses:

Zeus	King of the Gods
Hera	Queen of the Gods
Poseidon	God of the Seas
Athena	Goddess of Wisdom and War
Apollo	God of Light and Truth
Aphrodite	Goddess of Love

A good book to start with is *The Olympians,* by Leonard Everett Fisher (Holiday House, 1984). After learning about the gods and goddesses, your students can write about their favorite ones or make up their own mythological tales.

Name _____

Build the Pillars of the Parthenon

Directions: Build the Parthenon
by filling in the blanks on the pillars
to complete the sentences.

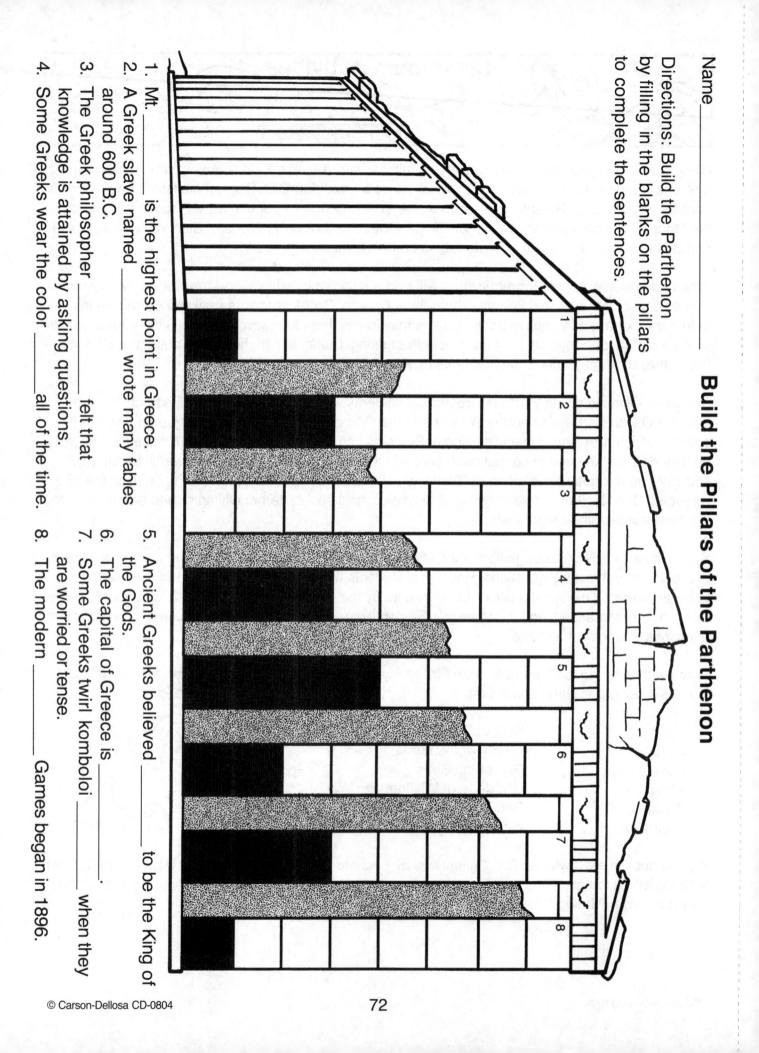

1. Mt. _____ is the highest point in Greece.
2. A Greek slave named _____ wrote many fables around 600 B.C.
3. The Greek philosopher _____ felt that knowledge is attained by asking questions.
4. Some Greeks wear the color _____ all of the time.
5. Ancient Greeks believed _____ to be the King of the Gods.
6. The capital of Greece is _____.
7. Some Greeks twirl komboloi _____ when they are worried or tense.
8. The modern _____ Games began in 1896.

72

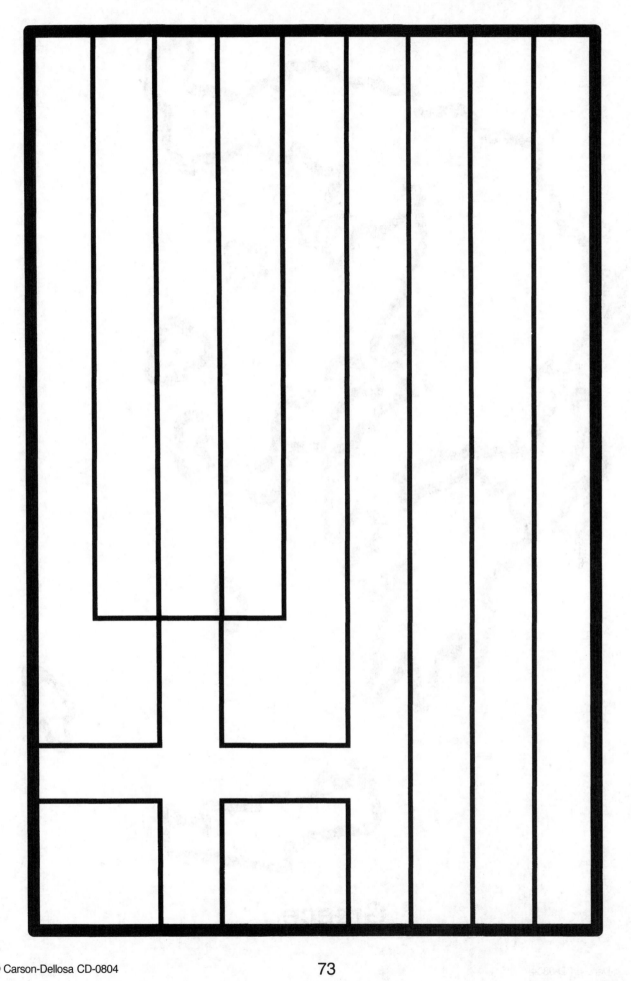

The Flag of Greece

Greece

Teacher Resources

Caselli, Giovanni. *A Greek Potter.* Peter Bedrick Books, 1986.

Dubois, Jill. *Greece.* Benchmark Books, 1995.

Elliott, Drossoula and Sloan. *We Live in Greece.* Hodder Wayland, 1985.

Fisher, Leonard Everett. *Olympians: Great Gods and Goddesses of Ancient Greece.* Holiday House, 1984.

Hollinger, Peggy. *Greece.* Bookwright Press, 1990.

Honan, Linda. *Spend the Day in Ancient Greece: Projects that Bring the Past to Life.* Jossey-Bass, 1998.

Jacobsen, Karen. *Greece.* Children's Press, 1990.

Lye, Keith. *Take a Trip to Greece.* Franklin Watts, 1983.

Nardo, Don. *Ancient Greece.* Greenhaven Press, 2000.

Pearson, Anne. *Ancient Greece. DK Children's Publishing*, 2004.

Stein, R. Conrad. *Greece.* Children's Press, 1987.

Waterlow, Julia. *Greece.* Bookwright Press, 1992.

Williams, Susan. *The Greeks.* Thomson Learning, 1993.

Wright, Rachel. *Greeks: Facts, Things to Make, Activities.* Franklin Watts, 1993.

Approaching Italy

Area: 116,320 sq. miles
Capital City: Rome
Population: 62,137,802
Main Language(s): Italian
Main Religion(s): Roman Catholicism
Currency: Euro
Government: Parlimentary Democracy
Flag:

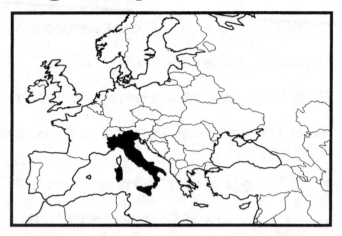

Adopted in 1870, the Italian flag was first used in 1796 by Italians who supported Napoleon of France during a war against Austria. Napoleon designed the flag to look like that of France, but substituted green, his favorite color, for the blue of the French flag.

For Your Information

Italy, a country in southern Europe, is known for its rich cultural heritage and natural beauty. Its cities have impressive churches, large central plazas, and museums that contain some of the world's best-known art. The country's Alpine ski slopes, sunny seaside resorts, historic cities, and world famous architecture have made Italy a leading tourist nation.

Italy acquired its name from the ancient Romans. The Romans called the southern part of the peninsula *Italia,* meaning "land of oxen" or "grazing land." The country boasts several world-famous cities. Rome, the capital and largest city of Italy, was the center of the Roman Empire 2,000 years ago. Florence was the home of many artists of the Renaissance, a period of great achievement in the arts. Venice, with its complex canal system, attracts tourists from all over the world.

More than two-thirds of Italy's people live in urban areas. Most Italians live in concrete apartments. A few wealthy people live in single-family homes. Many residents buy rather than rent their apartments. Poor neighborhoods are usually located on the outskirts of the cities.

Italians take great pride in the quality of their cooking. They eat their main meal between noon and 3:00 p.m. Antipasti, or "appetizers," are usually served first. Then, a pasta or soup dish is served accompanied by crusty bread cut from long, thin loaves (no butter). The second course is usually a meat dish served with a green salad. The meal is followed with fruit, cheeses, and sometimes dessert. The most popular meats are veal and pork. Pizza is a popular snack and is also eaten as a light meal. Traditionally, wine is served with every meal except breakfast.

Italians enjoy a wide variety of sports. Soccer is the most popular sport in Italy. Every major city has a professional soccer team, but soccer is not just a spectator sport--on weekends Italy's parks are filled with children and adults playing the game. Basketball is also very popular.

Fascinating Facts

 Pisa, Italy, is home to the famous leaning tower which is part of a beautiful church. When workmen began building the bell tower, it began to lean and sink. After many years, they continued to work on the tower, building it as straight as they could. The tower leaned even more, and today the tower leans almost ten feet to one side and is continuing to slowly sink into the ground.

 The smallest country in Europe is actually contained within the city of Rome. It is called the Vatican City and is home to the pope, who is head of the Catholic church. Huge crowds gather outside the world's largest church, Saint Peter's, and cheer *il Papa!* ("The Pope!") when the pope appears at the window.

 Opera music is very popular in Italy. Opera is a special kind of theater in which people sing, rather than speak their lines. There are opera houses in all parts of Italy. Italians cheer madly when they hear a beautiful voice. They also boo when they think the singing is not quite good enough. Italians once booed one of the greatest tenors in history, Enrico Caruso, off the stage because he missed a high note.

 The island of Sicily is only a short distance from Africa. Occasionally, a hot wind from the Sahara Desert called a *sirocco* blows across the Mediterranean Sea to Italy. The wind carries with it a red dust. If it rains, the rain is red. Many Italians believe the sirocco puts them in a bad mood.

 On the day before Easter in Florence, Italy, a famous display takes place each year called *Scoppio del Carro* or "Explosion of the Cart." After two solemn days of mourning the death of Jesus, a rocket shaped like a dove is lit at the church altar. It shoots along a wire and through the doors of the church to the car. The crowds cheer wildly as the car explodes, signifying Jesus rising from the dead.

 Italians love soccer as well as snow skiing, bicycle racing, and all types of water sports. Basketball is gaining in popularity in Italy, and competitive leagues are popping up all over the country. To improve the quality of play, the Italian basketball leagues passed a rule allowing each team to hire one foreign player. These new players were nearly always Americans. The fans were so pleased with the higher level of play that now two foreign players are allowed on each team. Coaches are often sent to the United States to find tall centers and forwards.

 Italy has several active volcanos. Near the city of Naples, a volcano named *Vesuvius* occasionally erupts, spilling hot lava on the towns below. At the foot of Vesuvius lies the ancient city of Pompeii. In 79 A.D., the mountain erupted and buried the town in hot lava and ash. Two hundred years ago, scientists began to dig out the remains of the city. They found houses, shops, and bakeries with bread still in the ovens. It is not surprising that both *lava* and *volcano* are Italian words.

Language Activities

Italian Numbers

uno (OO-noh)	one
due (OOO-eh)	two
tre (TREH)	three
quattro (KWAHT-troh)	four
cinque (CHEEN-kweh)	five
sei (SAY)	six
sette (SEHT-teh)	seven
otto (OHT-toh)	eight
nove (NOH-veh)	nine
dieci (DYEH-chee)	ten

Roman Numerals

I	one
II	two
III	three
IV	four
V	five
VI	six
VII	seven
VIII	eight
IX	nine
X	ten

Italian Days of the Week

lunedi (loo-nay-DEE)	Monday
martedi (mahr-tay-DEE)	Tuesday
mercoledi (mehr-coh-lay-DEE)	Wednesday
giovedi (jee-oh-vay-DEE)	Thursday
venerdi (vay-nayr-DEE)	Friday
sabato (SAH-bah-toh)	Saturday
domenica (doh-MAY-nee-kah	Sunday

Italian Colors

rosso (ROHS-soh)	red
arancione (ah-rahn-chee-OH-nay)	orange
giallo (Jee-AHL-loh)	yellow
verde (VAYR-day)	green
blu (BLOO)	blue
bianco (bee-AHN-koh)	white
nero (NAY-roh)	black

Everyday Italian Expressions

Buon giorno (Buohn JOHR-noh)	hello
Arriverderci (Ah-REE-veh-dehr-chee)	goodbye
Ti voglio bene (Tee VOH-glioh BEH-neh)	I love you.
Per favore (Pehr FAH-voh-reh)	please
Grazie (GRAH-zyeah)	thank you
Sí (SEE)	yes
No (NOH)	no
Mi dispiace (Mee Dee-SPEEAH-che)	I'm sorry.
Mi chiamo (Mee KHIA-moh)	My name is ...

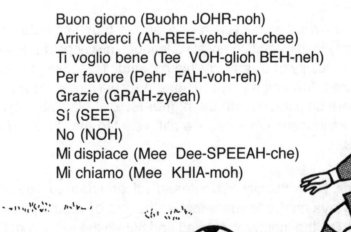

Italian Spaghetti Sauce

Ingredients:
2 tablespoons butter
1 onion, chopped
1 clove garlic, peeled and cut in half
1 35 oz. can of tomatoes
2 tablespoons tomato paste
½ teaspoon salt
½ teaspoon oregano
½ teaspoon basil
¼ teaspoon pepper

Directions:
Heat the butter in a saucepan. Add the onion and garlic. Cook for 5-10 minutes until the onion is pale yellow. Remove the garlic. Add the tomatoes and crush them as they cook, using a fork and a spoon. Add the tomato paste and seasonings. Cook uncovered for 20-30 minutes. Serve over different kinds of cooked pasta.

Gelato (Italian Ice)

Italians love ice cream. In fact, they invented it! *Gelato* is sold on city streets from specially made motorcycle carts. Ancient Romans made iced wines and fruit juices and learned how to preserve ice in the summer. Ices have been popular in Italy ever since and enjoyed in other countries, too.

Ingredients:
4 cups water
2½ cups sugar
2 cups orange, lemon,
     or cranberry juice

Directions:
In a medium saucepan, bring water and sugar to boil. Stir until sugar is dissolved. Boil for five minutes, stirring often. Remove from heat and cool thoroughly. Stir in juice. Pour into a freezer container and freeze for 4-5 hours. Stir occasionally until mixture is almost completely frozen. Spoon into small cups and serve with spoons.

Classroom Activities

Two of the world's greatest artists were Italians. Michelangelo Buonarroti made wonderful statues and Leonardo da Vinci painted the *Mona Lisa* and *The Last Supper.* Leonardo also tried for years to design a machine that could fly and a modern-day battle tank. Because Leonardo wrote his notes backwards, they have to be read with a mirror. Share with your students some of the artwork of Michelangelo and Leonardo de Vinci. Students can paint their own "masterpieces" for a classroom art gallery or try writing backwards like Leonardo.

Italians love pastamore than 500 types, each having its own shape. Some of the names of the pastas are clever reminders of their shape. **Linguine** is "little tongues;" **farfalle** is "butterflies;" **bucatini** is "little holes;" **agnolotti** is "little fat lambs;" and **tortellini** is "little twists." Have a "Pasta Party" in your classroom. Each student can bring a bag or box of pasta to school. Children can sort the different kinds of pasta, string some for necklaces, or create pictures using only pasta, paper, and glue. Save some of the pasta to cook with homemade tomato sauce (see the recipe on page 79).

Almost everyone loves Italian food, and it is popular in many parts of the world. Have an Italian feast in your classroom with dishes brought from home. Top off the feast with homemade Italian ice (see the recipe on page 79).

Each region and city of Italy is unique in its own right. Italian cities such as Venice, Florence, Milan, Naples, Palermo, and Rome have distinct characteristics and are fascinating places to visit. Working with partners or in groups, have your students select an Italian city, research five facts about it, and find its location on a map of Italy (see the map on page 83). Students can share their information with the class.

Famous operas such as *Madame Butterfly* and *La Boheme* are very much a part of Italy's history. Play for your students different selections of opera music or songs by the popular Italian tenor, Luciano Pavarotti. Do your students like this type of music? How does it make them feel?

Italian children must go to school on Saturdays and wear uniforms or smocks to protect their clothes. Most schools do not have playgrounds or school sports. However, many schools end the day at 12:30. In Italy, all of the time spent in school is devoted to schoolwork. Games and sports must wait until afterward. In most Italian schools, students stand when a teacher enters the room as a sign of respect and call their teacher **maestro** or "master." Have your students write what they like and dislike about school. How would they feel about having a short day if recess, lunch, and games were not included?

Using just their fingers, Italians play a game called **morra.** Have students work with a partner and try their hand at this fast and popular Italian game. Here's how to play: Two players face each other and quickly show any number of fingers on one hand. At the same moment, each calls out a number. If the number equals the total of fingers on the other player's hand, the player who said it is the winner. Morra is especially fun when the game gets faster and faster.

Name _____

Tower of Pisa Word Search

Directions: Find the twelve words from the word list in the puzzle. Circle the words as you find them. They are written across, down, and diagonally.

Word List

- pasta
- opera
- Sicily
- antipasto
- Venice
- spaghetti
- Catholic
- Rome
- Michelangelo
- soccer
- Pisa
- volcano

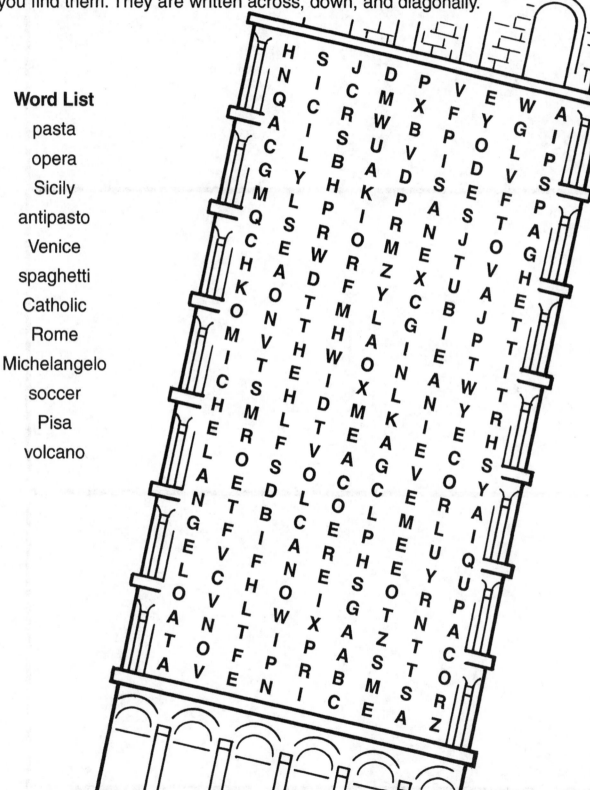

The Flag of Italy

Italy

Teacher Resources

Biucchi, Edwina. *Italian Food and Drink.* Franklin Watts, 1987.

Borlenghi, Patricia. *Italy.* Franklin Watts, 1995.

Clark, Colin. *Journey Through Italy.* Troll Associates, 1994.

Gidal, Sonya and Gidal, Tim. *My Village in Italy.* Pantheon Books, 1962.

Haskins, James. *Count Your Way Through Italy.* Carolrhoda Books, 1990.

Hubley, Penny. *A Family in Italy.* Lerner Publications Company, 1987.

James, Ian. *Inside Italy.* Franklin Watts, 1988.

Mariella, Cinzia. *Passport to Italy.* Franklin Watts, 1994.

Peterson, Christine and David. *Italy (True Books).* Children's Press, 2002.

Powell, Jillian. *Italy.* Bookwright Press, 1991.

Powell, Jillian. *What's It Like to Live in Italy?* Waterbird Press, 2003.

Sansone, Emma. *Italy and Italian.* Barron's Educational Series, 1993.

Sproule, Anna. *Italy.* Silver Burdett Press, 1987.

Stein, R. Conrad. *Italy: the Land and Its People.* Children's Press, 1984.

Travis, David. *The Land and People of Italy.* HarperCollins, 1992.

Winter, Jane Kohen. *Italy.* Benchmark Books, 1995.

Next Stop...France

Area: 212,935 sq. miles
Capital City: Paris
Population: 67,106,161
Main Language(s): French
Main Religion(s): Roman Catholicism
Currency: Euro
Government: Parlimentary Democracy
Flag:

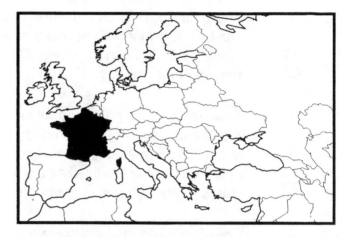

The French flag is called the tricolor. In 1789, King Louis XVI first used its three colors (blue, white, and red) to represent France.

For Your Information

France, the largest Western European country in area, is shaped like a hexagon, and three of its six sides are bounded by water. The English Channel is on the northwest, the Atlantic Ocean and Bay of Biscay are on the west, and the Mediterranean Sea is on the southeast. Paris, the capital and largest city of France, is one of the world's great cities. For hundreds of years, Paris has been a world capital of art and learning. Many great artists have produced their finest masterpieces there. Every year, millions of tourists visit such famous Paris landmarks as the Cathedral of Notre Dame, the Eiffel Tower, and the Louvre, one of the largest art museums in the world.

There is much more to France, however, than just Paris. The snow-capped Alps form the border between France and Italy. Sunny beaches and steep cliffs stretch along the French coast on the Mediterranean Sea. Fishing villages dot the Atlantic coast of northwestern France. Colorful apple orchards, dairy farms, and vineyards lie throughout much of the French countryside. The peaceful, wooded Loire Valley has many chateaux or "castles."

The French are famous for their enjoyment of life. Good food and good wine are an important part of everyday living for most French. The wines of France are considered by many to be the best in the world. Almost every restaurant and area has at least one special recipe of its own. The delicious breads, appetizers, sauces, soups, and desserts of France are copied by cooks all over the world.

France is not only a beautiful and historic country, it is also rich and powerful. France has great automobile, chemical, and steel industries. A leader in growing wheat, vegetables, and many other crops, France stands fifth among the countries of the world in its trade with other nations. In addition, France plays an important part in world politics. Its foreign policies affect millions of people in other countries. The political importance of France today resulted partly from the leadership of Charles de Gaulle, who served as president of the country from 1958 to 1969. De Gaulle looked on France as a world power and followed a policy that was independent of both the United States and Russia.

Fascinating Facts

The Eiffel Tower is one of Paris' most famous landmarks. It was built in 1889 by Gustave Eiffel for the International Exposition. It is 984 feet high and, until 1930, it was the tallest building in the world. On a clear day, it is possible to see over 40 miles from the top of the tower.

The French enjoy gathering wild mushrooms and *truffles* from fields and woodlands. A truffle is a kind of underground mushroom that is considered a delicacy and is very expensive. Sometimes a pet pig or dog is trained to sniff out underground truffles. Any newly discovered truffle sites are kept a closely guarded secret because they can be sold for very high prices at market.

French is a beautiful language that is flowing and harmonious to hear. Over the years, the French have borrowed many words from English, such as "le parking," "le weekend," "le businessman," and "le babysitting." Some people feared that the French language would be corrupted and weakened by the use of too many foreign words. A law now forbids the official use of English words where there is already a French word in existence.

The French love to watch and play all kinds of sports. Swimming pools or sports halls at the *maison des jeunes* (youth clubs) are common places for children to meet. Along with soccer and rugby, the French enjoy following professional bicycle racing. Every July, France hosts the *Tour de France*, a three-week bicycle race. The punishing race covers a distance of over 2,000 miles over some of the highest, steepest mountain passes in France. The cyclist with the best time at the end of a day's racing is given a yellow jersey to wear the following day.

All over France children have fun with *Poisson d' avril* or "April Fish," which is an April Fool's trick. Children try to pin a paper fish on someone's back without being noticed. They then point and laugh at the person and call out, "Poisson d' avril!"

In 1940 in southern France, several boys went hunting and suddenly were unable to find their dog. They found him barking from a hole in the ground which was part of a huge cave. In the cave they found over 500 paintings of horses, bison, reindeer, and other wild animals. These paintings were made by cavemen more than 15,000 years ago! Historians believe that the caves and their drawings were used for magic and ancient religious rites.

To the French, cooking is an art and greatly adds to the enjoyment of life. They take great pride and pleasure in cooking, and their chefs and cuisine are world famous. The French believe that good food deserves fresh ingredients, time, and attention. It is not only important to cook well in France, but to shop well, too. When shopping, the French can be very demanding and choose their goods with care. They would not hesitate to return a rotten apple or a slightly damaged item to the shopkeeper.

Language Activities

French Numbers

un (uhn)	one
deux (duh)	two
trois (trwah)	three
quatre (kah-truh)	four
cinq (sank)	five
six (seess)	six
sept (seht)	seven
huit (weet)	eight
neuf (nuhf)	nine
dix (deess)	ten

French Colors

rouge (roozh)	red
orange (o-ronzh)	orange
jaune (zhohn)	yellow
vert (vair)	green
bleu (bluh)	blue
violet (veeh-o-lay)	purple
blanc (blon)	white
rose (rohz)	pink
brun (bruhn)	brown
noir (nwahr)	black

Tete, Epaules, Genoux Et Pieds

Tete, epaules, genoux et pieds,
genoux et pieds. (repete)
J'ai deux yeux, un nez, une bouche,
et deux oreilles.
Tete, epaules, genoux, et pieds,
genoux et pieds.

Head, Shoulders, Knees and Feet

Sung to the tune of "Head, Shoulders, Knees and Toes"
Head, shoulders, knees and feet,
knees and feet. (repeat 2 times)
I have two eyes, one nose, one mouth,
and two ears.
Head, shoulders, knees and feet,
knees and feet.

Frère Jacques*

Fre - re   Jac - ques, fre - re Jac - ques, dor-mez-vous,   dor-mez-vous
Bro - ther Ja - cob, bro - ther Ja -cob,   are you sleeping, are you sleeping?

Son-nez les ma-ti-nes, son-nez les ma-ti-nes.   Din, din, don!   Din, din, don!
Ring the mor-ning bells, ring the morn-ing bells. Ding, ding, dong!   Ding, ding, dong!

* based on *Frere Jacques,* by Barbara Hazen, Lippincott, 1973

French Recipes

French Hot Chocolate

Children love to drink this chocolate treat in the morning with a French baguette or a tasty croissant.

Ingredients:
2 oz. semisweet baking chocolate
4 cups whole milk
⅓ cup sugar
 cocoa powder to sprinkle

Directions:
Break chocolate into pieces in a saucepan and add ½ cup of milk. Heat on the stove, stirring often until the chocolate and milk are smooth. Bring to just boiling. Stir in the rest of milk and heat through. Add sugar to taste. Remove from heat and pour into a mug. Sprinkle cocoa powder on top and enjoy!

Casse-croûte (A French snack)

Ingredients:
 2 slices of bread
 1 slice of Gruyere cheese
 1 slice of ham
 1 tablespoon butter

Directions:
Make a sandwich with the bread, cheese, and ham. Spread butter on both sides of the sandwich and place in a frying pan. *Sauté* (fry gently) on both sides until sandwich is slightly brown and cheese is melted. Bon appetit!

Chocolate Truffles

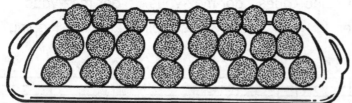

Ingredients:
6 oz. unsweetened chocolate
1 cup butter
4 teaspoons heavy cream
1 cup confectioners' sugar
4 tablespoons nuts, finely chopped
cocoa powder

Directions:
In a saucepan over low heat, melt the chocolate and butter. Stir in the cream and gradually add the sugar and nuts. Then, stir constantly until mixture is smooth. Transfer to a bowl then cover and refrigerate several hours. When the chocolate mixture is firm, form into small balls with your hands. Roll the balls in cocoa until covered. Store the chocolate truffles in the refrigerator.

Classroom Activities

The women of Paris are said to be among the best dressed in the world. Many people look to Paris every season for new styles of fashionable clothes. Fashion houses such as Chanel, Hermes, and Yves St. Laurent produce beautiful clothing which is sold throughout the world. Let your students design on paper a new style of clothes for school, sports, or for dressy occasions. You can also have a class fashion show. Students can wear a favorite outfit to school and write a detailed description to be read as they walk down a classroom "runway."

With more than eight miles of galleries, **Musée de Louvre** (the "Louvre Museum") in Paris is one of the most famous museums in the world. Originally a royal palace, the Louvre now houses famous paintings such as Leonardo da Vinci's *Mona Lisa* and the Greek sculptures *Venus de Milo* and the *Winged Victory*. Turn your classroom into the Louvre Museum. Using different types of mediums (paint, mosaics, clay, etc.), have your students create their own "masterpieces." They can title their artworks and write descriptions of their work.

From 1870 into the 1900s, a group of painters including Claude Monet, Edouard Manet, and Auguste Renoir changed people's ideas of paintings. Unlike most artists at that time, these men were more interested in using light to capture images and the "impression" of a scene rather than exact copies of what they saw. To achieve this, the "impressionist" painters avoided neat outlines and painted in dabs and dashes. Colors were mixed right on the canvas rather than on the palettes. Have your students try their own paintings in the style of impressionism. Let each student wet down a white piece of construction paper and quickly apply paint in dabs and dashes.

The French often boast that they can offer 365 different cheeses, one for every day of the year. Using milk from cows, ewes, and goats, popular cheeses such as Brie, Roquefort, and Camembert are exported to most countries of the world. Have a cheese-tasting party in your classroom with samples for the children to try. Let your students respond to different cheeses with a graph, a chart, or journal responses. Which cheese did they like the best? Which was their least favorite?

Similar to bowling, a popular French game is **boules.** The game is played on flat ground and nearly every town in France has a shady area set aside for playing. Spectators often gather around the game to give advice about throwing or how to knock the other players' metal boules out of the way. Have your students try playing boules using tennis balls or softballs. To play the game, each player throws two boules (balls), one at a time, at a **cochonnet** (a smaller ball). The thrower of the boule that lands nearest to the cochonnet wins.

In 1824, when only 15 years old, a blind Frenchman named Louis Braille developed a reading and writing system for the blind. Raised dots were used to form letters. Introduce the Braille system of reading to your students by using materials found at your local library or by inviting a guest speaker to your classroom.

Perfumed Beads

The perfume made in France is well known throughout the world. Many of the major fashion houses create and sell their own brands of perfume such as Chanel, Dior, and Givenchy. By using locally grown jasmine, violets, lavender, and other imported flowers, France has had a large perfume industry since the sixteenth century. Create a homemade and *chic*, or "smart," strand of perfumed beads.

Materials:
- 6 handfuls of dried chamomile flowers or rose petals
- medium saucepan
- water
- blender or food processor
- colander with tiny holes
- cookie sheet
- needle string

1	2	3
Place the dried flowers in the saucepan and add just enough water to cover them.	Simmer on low heat for one hour (do not boil). Add a little more water to cover petals if the water level drops.	Pour the flowers and water into a blender and mix for 1-2 minutes.
		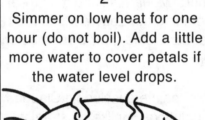

4	5	6
Scoop the mixture into a colander. Squeeze out the excess water with your hands.	Roll the mixture into small beads and place on a cookie sheet.	Place the beads in a warm place (sunny window) to dry for 3-4 days.

7

When the beads are dry, carefully push the needle through each bead.
String the beads to make a sweet-smelling necklace or bracelet.
Store beads in an airtight container.

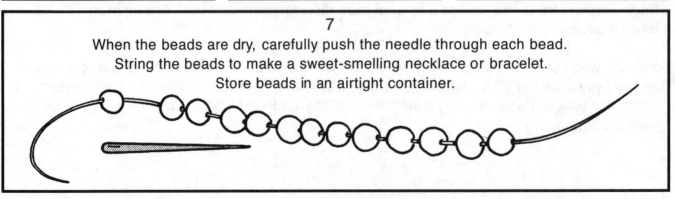

French Puzzle

Across

2. The capital of France is _____ .
4. The _____ Tower is a famous monument in Paris.
6. France is known throughout the world for its wine and delicious_____ .
7. Many chateaux are found in the _____ Valley.

Down

1. Between 1870 and the early 1900s, _____ paintings became popular in France.
3. The Tour de France is a popular _____ race.
5. The snow-capped _____ are part of the border between France and Italy.

The Flag of France

France

93

Teacher Resources

Behnke, Alison. *France in Pictures.* Lerner Publications, 1991.

Bender, Lionel. *France.* Silver Burdett, 1988.

Gamgee, John. *Journey Through France.* Troll Associates, 1994.

Ganeri, Anita. *France.* Franklin Watts, 1993.

Ganeri, Anita. *France and the French.* Gloucester Press, 1993.

Gofen, Ethel. *France.* Benchmark Books, 2003.

James, Ian. *Inside France.* Franklin Watts, 1989.

Moss, Peter. *France.* Children's Press, 1993.

Norbrook, Dominique. *Passport to France.* Franklin Watts, 1994.

Pluckrose, Henry Arthur. *France: Picture a Country.* Franklin Watts, 1999.

Somerville, Louisa. *The Usborne First Book of France.* Educational Development Corporation, 1989.

Sookram, Brian. *France.* Chelsea House, 1997.

Sturges, Jo. *France.* Crestwood House, 1993.

A Visit to Russia

Area: 6,592,850 sq. miles
Capital City: Moscow
Population: 142,257,519
Main Language(s): Russian
Main Religion(s): Russian Orthodox Church
Currency: Ruble
Goverment: Federation
Flag:

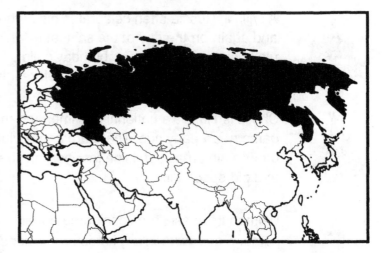

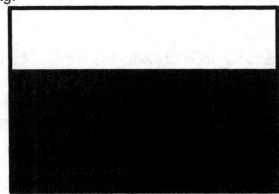

Adopted in 1991, the Russian flag is a tricolor: three equal bands of white (top), blue (middle), and red (bottom). It had been the unofficial ethnic flag of the Russian people since 1988.

For Your Information

Russia, located on two continents, Europe and Asia, is the world's largest country in area. It is almost twice as big as Canada, the second largest country. From 1922 until 1991, Russia was the largest republic in the Soviet Union, the most powerful Communist country in the world. The Soviet Union fell apart in 1991. After the breakdown, Russia began to set up a new political, legal, and economic system.

In August, 1991, after an attempted coup against President Mikhail Gorbachev by Communist party loyalists, the new Russian Parliament voted to dissolve the Soviet Union and to disband the Communist Party. The Commonwealth of Independent States is an economic union that was formed in December, 1991, in which each state or republic has its own government. It consists of Russia and many of the original Soviet republics. Boris Yeltsin was elected the first president of Russia in 1991. The second president, Vladimir Putin, was elected in 1999.

Most of Russia's people are ethnic Russians (descendants of early Slavic people). More than 100 minority nationalities also live in Russia. The Russian people are used to hardship and change, but they are strong of spirit and warm of heart. About three-fourths of the people make their homes in urban areas.

Russia has abundant natural resources, including extensive deposits of petroleum, natural gas, coal, gold, and iron ore. Many of these reserves lie far from settled areas. Russia's severe, cold climate makes it difficult to take advantage of many of the country's valuable resources.

Russia made many great contributions to the arts during the 1800s. Such authors as Anton Chekhov, Fyodor Dostoevsky, and Leo Tolstoy wrote masterpieces of literature. Russian composers, including Peter Tchaikovsky, Modest Mussorgsky, and Nikolai Rimsky-Korsakov, created music of lasting greatness. Russians also make valuable artistic contributions in the fields of architecture, ballet, and painting .

Fascinating Facts

A child in Russia often celebrates his birthday twice a year, once on the day of his birth and again on the day of the saint after which he is named. Instead of a cake, a birthday pie is more common. The birthday child's name and a short greeting are written on the pie by pricking holes in the crust before it is baked.

Chess is Russia's national pastime, and many children learn to play the difficult board game at an early age. There are chess clubs in schools, offices, and factories. City parks often have areas set aside for open-air chess games which attract large crowds of young and old spectators.

Women in Russia are considered equal to men, and most of them work outside of the home. Many women are in top professions, and girls are encouraged to become doctors, scientists, and engineers. Women comprise over half of Russia's doctors. Although their pay is equal to men, the salaries are not large. Doctors work very long hours, and they do not have the medicines and technology that are available in the United States.

On March 8, Russians celebrate International Women's Day. All men (fathers, sons, and husbands) do extra chores and give gifts to honor the women in their lives. Offices and schools are closed for the holiday.

When a child loses a tooth in Russia, he or she looks forward to the "Tooth Mouse." Before going to sleep, the child will place the tooth underneath the bed. If it is gone in the morning, a new tooth will be sure to replace the one now missing. Russian children also eagerly await the New Year when **Deuska Moroz** (Grandfather Frost) brings goodies and small presents.

Otherwise known as "The Blue Eye of Siberia," Lake Baikal is the largest lake in Russia and the oldest and deepest lake in the world. It holds one-fifth of the world's fresh water, but today it is threatened by pollution. An old legend states that a dip in Lake Baikal will make a person look one year younger.

Russia has had many firsts in space explorations. In 1957, Russia (then a part of the Soviet Union) launched the first artificial Earth satellite called **Sputnik 1.** A month later, they launched **Sputnik 2**, which carried a dog named Laika beyond Earth's atmosphere. Two years later, the Russian space probe **Luna 2** was first to land on the moon. In 1961, Yuri Gagarin became the first human being to orbit Earth in his spacecraft, **Vostok 1.**

Most Russian families have television sets, radios, and small appliances. Modern digital devices, however, are in great demand but are expensive and hard to find. The Russian telecommunication system is poorly developed. It can take months or even years to install telephones in new apartment complexes.

Language Activities

Russian Alphabet

Letter		Pronunciation	
А	а	AH	(as in father)
Б	б	BEH	(as in boy)
В	в	VEH	(as in vest)
Г	г	GEH	(as in girl)
Д	д	DEH	(as in desk)
Е	е	YEH	(as in yet)
Ё	ё	YO	(as in yonder)
Ж	ж	ZHE	(as in measure)
З	з	ZEH	(as in zeppelin)
И	и	EE	(as in week)
Й	й	YEE	(as in yield)
К	к	KAH	(as in karate)
Л	л	EL	(as in like)
М	м	EM	(as in might)
Н	н	EN	(as in now)
О	о	AW	(as in dog)
П	п	PEH	(as in pet)
Р	р	ERH	(as in rock, rolled "R")
С	с	ES	(as in song)
Т	т	TEH	(as in tell)
У	у	OO	(as in boo)
Ф	ф	EF	(as in fall)
Х	х	CHA	(as in Scottish loch)
Ц	ц	TSEH	(as in prints)
Ч	ч	CHEH	(as in choose)
Ш	ш	SHA	(as in shop)
Щ	щ	SHCHA	(as in fresh cheese)
Ъ	ъ	T'VYOR-day ZNAHK	(no English equivalent)
Ы	ы	I	(as in hill)
Ь	ь	myach-KYAY ZNAHK	(no English equivalent)
Э	э	EH	(as in end)
Ю	ю	YEW	(as in you)
Я	я	YAH	(as in yacht)

Russian Numbers

один	(ah-DEEN)	one
два	(DVAH)	two
три	(TREE)	three
четыре	(cheh-TI-reh)	four
пять	(PYAHT)	five
Шесть	(SHYEST)	six
семь	(SYEHM)	seven
восемь	(VAW-syehm)	eight
девятв	(DYEH-vyeht)	nine
десятв	(DYEH-syeht)	ten

Russian Words

здравствуйте	(ZORAH-stooy-tyeh)	hello
до сьидания	(dah svee0DAH-nee-yuh)	good-bye
пожалуйста	(pah-ZHAHL-stuh)	please
спасибо	(spah-SEE-buh)	thank you
да	(DAH)	yes
нет	(NYEHT)	no
мама	(MAH-mah)	mother
папа	(PAH-pah)	father
Бабушка	(BAH-bush-kah)	grandmother
дедушка	(DYEH-doosh-kah)	grandfather

Russian Recipes

Pirog (Russian Apple Pie)

Ingredients:
4   apples
3   eggs
1   cup sugar
1   cup flour
1   teaspoon margarine

Directions:
Peel apples, cut into small pieces, and set aside. In a large bowl, mix together eggs, sugar, and flour. Grease a pie dish with margarine and fill the dish with the apples. Pour the egg mixture over the apples. Bake at 375° for 40 minutes or until apples are golden brown.

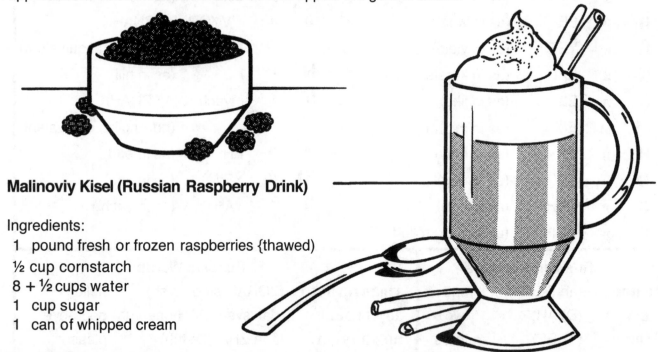

Malinoviy Kisel (Russian Raspberry Drink)

Ingredients:
1   pound fresh or frozen raspberries {thawed)
½ cup cornstarch
8 + ½ cups water
1   cup sugar
1   can of whipped cream

Directions:
Place the raspberries in a large bowl and crush them well with a spoon. Set aside. In a small bowl, mix together the cornstarch and ½ cup water until the cornstarch is dissolved. Set aside. In a large saucepan, combine 8 cups of water and sugar. Bring to a boil, stirring occasionally. Add crushed raspberries and the cornstarch mixture to the boiling syrup and stir until mixture begins to thicken. Remove the pan from the heat and let the drink cool to room temperature. Refrigerate until thoroughly chilled. Serve in a glass and top with whipped cream.

98

Classroom Activities

Russian grandmothers, **babushkas,** play an important role in the traditional Russian family. They look after the children and often do the family cooking and housework. This leaves both parents free to work. Celebrate grandmothers in your classroom by having a tea or luncheon, or invite some of the children's grandmothers or women from a nearby nursing home to your classroom to share their life stories. A student can also interview her parents to gather information on her "babushka" if she lives some distance away or is no longer living.

Russia is known for its beautifully decorated eggs called Faberge Eggs. The tradition began in 1884 with the Tsar of Russia, Alexander III, who wanted to give his wife the most beautiful Easter egg in the world. He hired a jeweler named Peter Faberge to design the egg. Faberge created the egg with white enamel, a gold yolk, and a tiny hen with eyes made from jewels sitting on top of the yolk. Every year after that, the royal family would commission a Faberge Easter egg costing thousands of dollars. Give each of your students large, white tagboard egg shapes. Have them decorate the eggs with markers, sequins, glitter, scraps of material, etc., to create their own Faberge eggs. You may want to have the children vote on the most beautifully decorated egg.

In Russia, everyone has three versions of his or her name, and one can usually tell by a last name if a person is male or female. Everybody is given a first name (girls' names always end with the letter **a**), but children are called by their nicknames. Adults are called by their first names plus the patronymic (a person's father's first name plus the masculine or feminine ending). Women and girls use a feminine ending; men and boys use a masculine ending. For example:

First Name	Nickname	With Patronymic	Last Name
*Nina (girl)	Niya	Nina Ivanovna	Masenkova
Yuri (boy)	Yura	Yuri Ivanovich	Masenkov
Olga (girl)	Olya	Olga Alexandrovna	Petrova
Vladimir (boy)	Volodya	Vladimir Alexandrov	Petrov

*Nina and Yuri are siblings, and Olga and Vladimir are siblings.

Have your students try writing their names the Russian way with three different versions: a first name, a nickname, and their first name with a patronymic.

Russia is the home of classical ballet, and there are over 40 major ballet companies. Some of the most famous Russian ballet dancers are Mikhail Baryshnikov, Rudolph Nureyev, and Anna Pavlova. Boys and girls begin ballet lessons when they are very young, and many dream of dancing someday with the famous Bolshoi Ballet. Teach your students the basic positions of ballet or invite a local dancer to your classroom to demonstrate ballet. You may want to play a recording of *The Nutcracker* ballet by the Russian composer Peter Tchaikovsky.

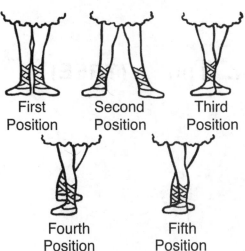

First Position Second Position Third Position Fourth Position Fifth Position

Counting Ballerinas

Directions: Read each Russian number word and count the number of ballerinas in each group. Draw a line to match each number word to the group with that many ballerinas in it. Then, color the ballerinas.

1. Два   **(DVAH)**

2. Четыре **(cheh-TI-ree)**

3. Один   **(ah-DEEN)**

4. Три   **(TREE)**

The Flag of Russia

Russia

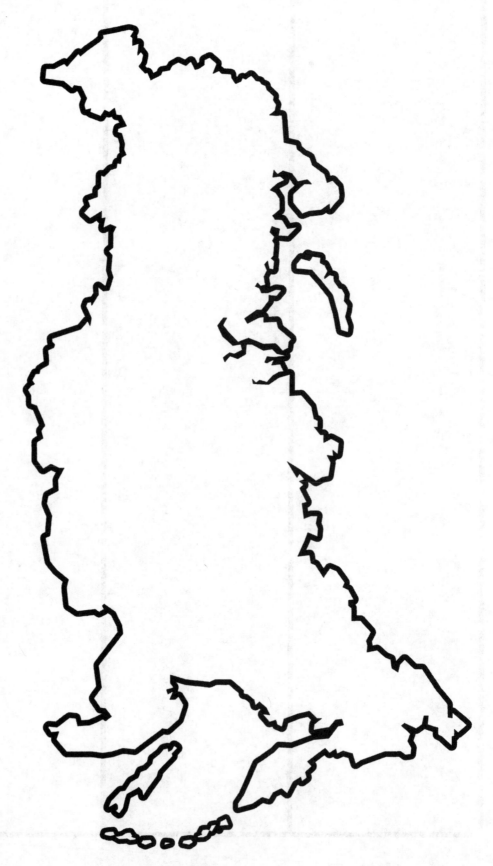

Teacher Resources

Berge, Anne, et al. *Russia ABCs: A Book About the People and Places of Russia.* Picture Window Books, 2004.

Carrion, Esther. *The Empire of the Czars.* Children's Press, 1994.

Flint, David. *Russian Federation.* Millbrook, 1992.

Harbor, Bernard. *The Breakup of the Soviet Union.* Wayland Publishers Ltd., 1992.

Jacobsen, Karen. *The Russian Federation.* Children's Press, 1994.

Kendall, Russ. *Russian Girl: Life in an Old Russian Town.* Scholastic, Inc., 1994.

Lapenkova, Valentina. *Russian Food and Drink.* Bookwright Press, 1988.

Lye, Keith. *Take a Trip to Russia.* Franklin Watts, 1982.

Murrell, Kathleen Berton. *Eyewitness: Russia.* OK Children's Publishing, 2000.

Plotkin, Gregory. *Cooking in the Russian Way.* Lerner Publishing Group, 2002.

Resnick, Abraham. *Commonwealth of Independent States.* Children's Press, 1993.

Torchinskii, 0. *Russia.* Marshall Cavendish, 1994.

Last Stop...India

Area: 1,269,346 sq. miles
Capital City: New Delhi
Population: 1,281,935,911
Main Language(s): Hindi, English, and Urdu
Main Religion(s): Hinduism and Islam
Currency: Rupee
Government: Federal Republic
Flag:

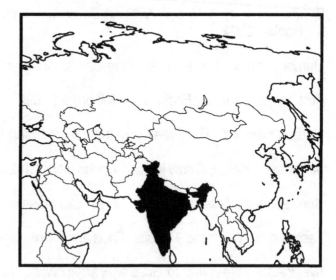

India's flag has three equal horizontal bands: deep saffron (for courage and sacrifice) at the top, white (for purity and truth) in the middle, and dark green (for faith and fertility) at the bottom. The wheel in the center is an ancient symbol called the Dharma Chakra (Wheel of Law).

For Your Information

India, a large country in southern Asia, is the second largest country in the world in population. Only China, its northeastern neighbor, has more people. About one out of every six people in the world lives in India.

India has great varieties and differences in both its land and its people. The land includes a desert, jungles, and one of the world's rainiest areas. In addition, India has broad plains, powerful rivers, the tallest mountains in the world, and tropical lowlands. The people in India belong to many different ethnic groups and religions. There are 16 major languages spoken there and more than 1,000 minor languages and dialects. Some Indians have great wealth; however, many others have only enough to spend a few cents a day on bare necessities. Some cannot afford shelter and must sleep in the streets. Some Indians are college graduates, yet many others have not attended school at all.

About 81 percent of the Indian people are Hindus, and about 13 percent are Muslims. The next largest religious groups, in order of their size, are Christians, Sikhs, Buddhists, and Jains. Religion plays a vital role in the Indian way of life. India's traditions are strongly rooted in religion and greatly influence their music, customs, dance, festivals, and clothing.

Clothing worn by Indians varies greatly by region. Members of the various religious groups may also dress differently. The Indians love to dress in colorful fabrics of silk and cotton. Some Indians, especially in the cities, wear Western-style clothing, but the clothing of many Indians consists of a long piece of cloth draped around the body. Many men wear a ***dhoti*** (a white garment wrapped between the legs). Most Indian women wear a ***sari*** (a straight piece of cloth draped around the body as a long dress).

Fascinating Facts

India is home to the smaller-eared Asiatic elephants, but their habitats are becoming scarce. They live mostly in northern India and travel in herds made up of one older male elephant, mature females, and young elephants of both sexes. Occasionally they are used as work animals in heavily wooded areas. Men called *mahouts* train the elephants to move and carry heavy logs.

Indian boys who practice the Sikh religion never cut their hair. When they turn five years old, they are given their first turban to wrap up their hair. On the other hand, Indian children who are part of the Hindu religion shave their heads when they are young, for it is believed to be unhealthy and unlucky to keep the hair with which you are born.

Family ties have great importance in India. Indians regard marriage as more of a relationship between two families than between two people. Young Indians generally are not allowed to date, and parents arrange most marriages; however, many young people have the right to reject any arrangements made by their parents. Many of the Indian households include not only parents and children but also the sons' wives as well as their children.

The *Taj Mahal* in northern India is one of the world's most magnificent buildings. The white marble monument was built more than 300 years ago by an emperor in memory of his wife. It took over 20,000 workers twenty-one years to build the Taj Mahal.

Indian women and girls love jewelry and often put a little round dot called a *bindi* in the middle of their foreheads. Women wear different colored bindis to match their clothes. Sometimes the color of the bindi will have a significant meaning. A white bindi is worn to show sadness or mourning, and red is worn for joyous occasions, such as weddings and celebrations.

India has the most trains and train stations, and its rail system carries the most passengers in the world. Ten million people travel by train each day. Only very wealthy Indians own cars, and in the major cities most people ride bicycles. In northwest India near Pakistan, however, the land is sandy and dry. Here, camels are the main means of transportation.

Dance is considered a serious art in India. In the 2,000-year-old *Bharat Natyam* dance, women use their hands, eyes, and positions of the neck to tell a story. Heavy makeup is worn to dramatize ancient characters.

When greeting each other, Indians do not shake hands. Rather, they fold their palms together and say *"Namaste'* ("I bow my head to you"). When meeting older relatives, Indians often touch their feet, for older people are greatly respected. White hair is a symbol of age and wisdom and is considered worthy of respect.

Indians love movies. In fact, India produces more films than any other country in the world. Going to the movies is a popular pastime, and traveling movie vans visit hundreds of villages to give outdoor film shows. Movies featuring singing and dancing are especially popular.

Language Activities

Hindi Expressions

Hindi	Pronunciation	Translation
नमस्ते	NA-mas-tay	hello (to one person)
नमस्कार	NA-mas-kar	hello (to a group)
हाँ	HAH	yes
नहीं	NA-HEE	no
कृपया	KREE-paya	please
शुक्रिया	SHU-kriya	thank you (to one person)
धन्यवाद	Dhan-ya-vaad	thank you (to a group)
क्या मैं मदद कर सकता हूँ ?	Kya-mane-maddat-kar SAKTA-Hoon?	Can I help?
मैं तुम से प्यार करता हूँ	may-tumse-PYAAR-Kar-ta Hoon.	I love you.
मेरा नाम है	mera-NAAM hai…	My name is ...

A Folktale from India*

Akbar, a great Indian emperor, had nine advisors in his court. His favorite advisor was named Birbal. He was a counselor, wise man, and jester to Akbar. Many stories are told about Birbal's wit, wisdom, and occasional silliness. Here is just one of the many folktales.

"Make It Shorter"

One day Akbar drew a line with his royal hand on the floor of the open court and commanded, "Make this line shorter, but don't by any means erase any part of it."

Everyone was stumped by this puzzle.

When it was Birbal's turn, he at once drew a longer line next to the first one. He didn't touch the first line.

Everyone in the court saw it and said, "That's true, the first line is shorter."

*Based on a story from *Folktales from India,* edited by A. K. Ramanujan, Pantheon Books, 1991.

Indian Recipes

Chapattis (Popular Unleavened Bread)

Ingredients:
4 cups whole meal flour
2 tablespoons vegetable oil
1 teaspoon salt
1 cup water

Directions:
In a large bowl mix the flour, oil, and salt. Gradually add the water to make a thick dough. Knead the dough and divide into twelve equal balls. Flatten each ball with a rolling pin and roll into a 5" circle. Fry on low heat, turning several times to avoid burning. As the chapattis cooks, it will puff. Serve warm and dip in butter, curries, or sauces.

Lassi (Yogurt Mint Drink)

Ingredients:
 1 quart milk
 1 quart plain yogurt
½ cup sugar
¼ cup honey
 4 teaspoons vanilla
 6 fresh mint stalks

Directions:
Mix together the milk, yogurt, sugar, honey, and vanilla. Pour into a pitcher and immerse mint into the lassi. Refrigerate overnight. Remove mint before serving.

Ahm Phul (Mango Whip Dessert)

Ingredients:
 2 ripe mangoes
½ cup milk
whipped cream

Directions:
Peel the mangoes, then cut the seeds from the flesh. Puree the mangoes in a blender and add the milk. Mix thoroughly. Serve in a frosted glass with a dab of whipped cream on top.

Families are extremely important to Indians, and brothers and sisters have a special relationship. Every year they celebrate their relationship with a festival called *Raksha Bandhan*. Girls tie a bracelet on their brothers' wrists. In return, boys promise to love, help, and protect their sisters forever. Have your students make a list of the things that make their brothers or sisters (or cousins) special. The children can use construction paper, beads, and interesting knickknacks to make bracelets for their siblings.

Children in India love to play **Kabbaddi**. To play the game, two teams face each other across a dividing line. The players in each team hold hands and stand in a line. A player from one team has to run across the dividing line and tag a player on the opposing team without being touched by the "enemy." The catch is that the player must do all of the running without taking a single breath, chanting "Kabbaddi, Kabbaddi, Kabbaddi" until the player gets back to his team. If the player gets to his line and is still chanting "Kabbaddi," all of the players who touched the runner are out of the game. So, the trick for the opposing team is to impede or surround the runner so that he cannot get back to his line before taking a breath. Play this fun game with your students during recess.

In October or November of each year, Hindu Indians celebrate **Diwali** (the "festival of lights"). During Diwali, thousands of lamps are placed along rooftops, roads, and outside houses to attract the blessing of **Lakshmi,** the goddess of good fortune.

In the hot fields of India, many farmers drape a white piece of fabric called a **dhoti** around their waists and between their legs. Most Indian women wear colorful **saris**. A sari is a long and beautiful piece of cloth which is wound around a woman. The loose end is placed over the head or shoulders. The easy-to-wear garment is made of cotton, nylon, or silk. Have your students bring to school 1½ yards of 3-foot-wide fabric. Boys can make dhotis to wear, and girls can follow the directions below to make a sari to wear for the day.

Name _____

Indian Crossword

Across:

2. Indian women wear long, beautiful _____ sari _____.
4. India celebrates _____, the "festival of lights," by placing lamps and lights on rooftops, roads, and the outside of houses.
5. Elephants are trained in India to carry _____ Logs _____ in heavily wooded areas.

Down:

1. _____ trains _____ are the most common form of transportation in India.
3. Most Indians practice the _____ Sikh _____ religion.

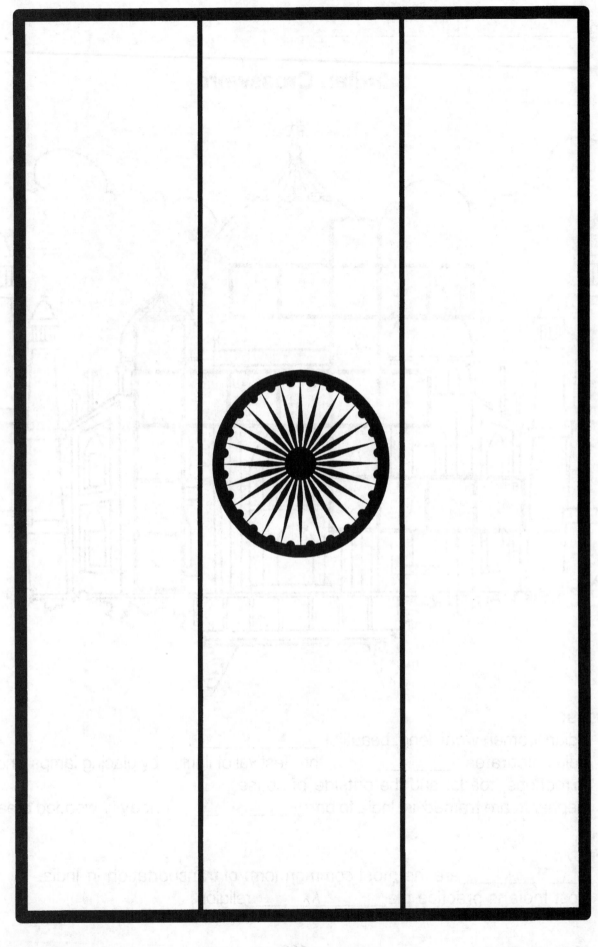

The Flag of India

India

Teacher Resources

Ardley, Bridgette. *India.* Silver Burdett, 1989.

Cumming, David. *India.* Hodder Children's Books, 2004.

Das, Prodeepta. *I Is for India.* Frances Lincoln, 2004.

Ganeri, Anita. *The India Subcontinent.* Franklin Watts, 1994.

Haskins, James. *Count Your Way through India.* Carolrhoda Books, 1992.

Kalman, Bobbie. *India: The People.* Crabtree, 2000.

Kanitkar V. P. *Indian Food and Drink.* Bookwright Press, 1987.

Lye, Keith. *Take a Trip to India.* Franklin Watts, 1982.

McNair, Sylvia. *India.* Children's Press, 1993.

Raman, T. A. *India.* The Fideler Company, 1983.

Sarin, Amita Vohra. *India: An Ancient Land, A New Nation.* Dillon Press, 1985.

Srinizasan, Radhika. *India.* Marshall Cavendish, 2001.

Stewart, Gail. *India.* Crestwood House, 1992.